Bug & Nona
on the go

Bug & Nona
on the go

Nona Freeman

Bug & Nona on the Go

by Nona Freeman

Cover Design by Tim Agnew

Printed in United States of America

Library of Congress Cataloging-in-Publication Data

Freeman, Nona, 1916-
    Bug & Nona on the go.

    1. Freeman, E. L. (Elpho Litris) 2. Freeman, Nona, 1916-
3. Missionaries—South Africa—Biography. 4. Missionaries—United States—
Biography—-I. Title. II. Title: Bug and Nona on the go.
BV3625.S67F73 1986   266'.0092'2 [B]   86-9845
ISBN 0-912315-27-X

To Bug
For love, faith, and laughter
lavishly given, I am forever grateful.
Nona

Contents

Introduction

Nudged by the Spirit, I have corralled these experiences from the reservoir of memory. These, and many more unrecorded incidents, have proved to us conclusively that walking hand in hand with Jesus is a beautiful way to live. Though our mistakes are myriad, the altogether lovely One makes none. He has a delightful touch of inspiration for all the events of life, both small and great, to make them profitable for instruction and guidance.

The writer of First Corinthians spoke of many types of voices, none without significance. We know that the voice of the redeemed lifts in song—

a song of love and forgiveness
a song of grace and rivers of life,
a song of deliverance and victory!
There can be only one theme for us —
". . . praising our Savior
all the day long."

Bug and Nona

PS: A personal note of gratitude to the unique family of the redeemed, who have blessed and helped me in countless ways.

N. F.

1

The Scorched Miracle

Sandra and Fred moved into our big house in Pretoria, South Africa. We built a small cottage on the same premises, which became our home base. We did not foresee what a convenient arrangement this would be until our missionary responsibilities were increased in 1971 to include the entire continent of Africa.

But circumstances change, and by 1976 this oldest daughter of ours and her family were making plans to move back to America. One day, while packing for one of our regular visits to Madagascar, I remembered something.

"Sandra, I haven't kept records as I should have, but I do remember keeping a diary for a few months back in 1948 when we were getting off to Africa. I've looked for it, but I haven't seen that little book in years. It would really be helpful when I start writing some more adventures. Will you please look carefully as you clean out shelves and drawers? It must be here somewhere."

"All right, Mother, I'll look. I remember there was such a book though I can't recall what it looked like."

She laid her sewing in her lap and looked at me

thoughtfully. "I can see it's important to you. I'll do more; I'll ask the Lord to help me find it. What color is it?"

"Once white, probably dingy gray by now."

When we returned from Madagascar, Sandra said, "Mother, I have a strange story to tell you. After you left, I looked everywhere for your diary, but no luck. I prayed again, and several days passed. Yesterday, I had a man cleaning out the garage where Daddy used to have his printing press. I told him to burn all those moldy samples and stacks of cut-offs and misprinted papers.

"I was sewing upstairs when suddenly the Lord spoke to me: 'Go see what has been thrown in the fire. Hurry!'

"I ran down the stairs and out to the back yard just as the African threw a book into the leaping flames. A rake lay nearby, so I grabbed it and pulled the book out of the fire."

There were tears in Sandra's eyes as she handed me the bedraggled diary.

"It's slightly scorched, but here's your miracle!"

Diary 1948 The New Year found us on our knees at the close of a precious watch night service. We had foot washing and communion. Even the

Jan. 1st children, Sandra, Dale, and Jerry, wept as they were moved by the Spirit. Five-year-old Lynda came to me with big tears in her eyes: "Mommy, my feet are also 'dutty'." So I washed them in the name of Jesus and asked Him to let those feet always walk the straight and narrow way.

(My mother, Carrie Eastridge, and three of my brothers, Joel, Paul, and Jerry, spent several days with us before returning to Gallup, New Mexico, where Mother is pioneering with the gospel among the Navajo Indians.)

Jan. 2nd   Mother and the boys left on the long trek home. It was not a sad parting though I have no idea when we'll see each other again. If God wills that our hopes and plans materialize, we will soon depart for Africa. It will have to be a pleasant experience, for service to Him is always sweet.

Tonight ended the first week of singing school with O.C. Thompson.

Jan. 3rd   The Covey Cooleys (near De Ridder) invited Brother Thompson and our family for a turkey dinner. It was like a little vacation—something we seldom have. There are so many things pressing to be ready for that long awaited sailing date. I wonder how I will feel when it actually happens. Probably it will seem like a dream.

Jan. 4th   I enjoyed teaching my class of young people this Sunday morning. Bug preached a super sermon on "The Power of the Church." Sweet worship in the evening service. Fletcher Lewis sang in the Spirit, and Sister Nash danced. I preached "The Morning Cometh, Also the Night."

Jan. 5th   We went to Leesville this afternoon for the final family group picture before we leave—I hope! I also went to the laundry in De Ridder to do a big washing. I do hope the Lord sends us one more day of sunshine tomorrow to dry all these clothes.

Bug went to a fellowship meeting at Pleasant View tonight.

Jan. 6th   Windy day and all the clothes are dry.

There is a possibility of sailing from New York. If that happens, I hope this springlike weather continues. Still, I prefer to believe the Lord will provide passage for us out of New Orleans.

Jan. 7th   My brother, John Martin, was in the Navy and went down with his ship when General MacArthur recaptured the Philippine Islands. It was just a short while after his nineteenth birthday. Johnny would have been twenty-two today. But considering everything, I would not call him back—even if it were in my power.

"Oh, Johnny, I remember how beautifully you sang 'Precious Jesus, Don't Forget.' My comfort is in knowing that you were *not* forgotten for one moment while you lived. And now you are with Him eternally."

"Precious Jesus, You will not forget me either. I only ask that You help me to be faithful."

Jan. 8th — A letter from the travel agency says sailing from New Orleans is unlikely for the next six months to a year. But I still believe that God is able to arrange it.

Jan. 9th — Life is certainly a rush! I'm having good opportunity of practicing what I've always preached: "I'd rather wear out for Jesus than rust out for the devil!"

Jan. 10th — My accordion arrived today. I sent Johnny Thomas the $150 I received for the old one. It was too big, and he found this one for me—a Scandali, 111 bass, sweet tone, small size—just what I've always wanted.

Jan. 11th — The Timothy Sonenbergs, who have a bur-den for Africa, spent part of the day with us. He taught my young people's class in a smooth, interesting lecture style.

Vanna's sister, Mary Edgerton, went with me to De Quincy for the night service. One young lady received the Holy Ghost. The saints there gave me more used clothing and canned fruit for Africa.

Jan. 12th — Bug went to Alexandria today to work on the campground. I packed the last barrel we have with used clothing. Need more barrels. Sharon is very sick tonight—acts almost like asthma. She hasn't been this way before.

"Lord, You are able!"

Jan. 13th   God bless Mary! She has ironed a basket of clothes I couldn't get done. My life seems composed of one long series of unfinished tasks. Somehow I need to learn to put first things *first*. But I must do the Lord's work even if I *never* get caught up with this housework and mending.

Jan. 14th   Mother wrote that if I will send her my watch, an Indian she has befriended will make me a lifetime silver band. So, I mailed it to her.

King-sized headache again. I phoned Bug—I shouldn't have. I guess I'm a baby.

Jan. 15th   I'm scheduled to begin my tour through East Texas, starting Saturday in Shreveport.

Jan. 16th   Sister Nash spent part of the day with me. Mary ironed another basket of clothes! Bug came home this afternoon. The weather is bad—cold rain, and it looks like it will turn to sleet. Only a few could make it out to church tonight. I wonder about tomorrow.

Jan. 17th   Dale has broken out with chicken pox! The wind is biting cold, with patches of snow here and there. I hated to take Lynda, Sharon, and the baby out in this weather. I decided once to cancel my East Texas trip but, after praying about it, changed my mind and caught the noon train. The snow increased as we traveled. Four inches in Shreveport. The children have taken colds.

Jan. 18th   I felt unusual liberty in the radio service. There was a good altar service after morning worship—two were filled with the Spirit. The offering was $100. Thank God—He knows our need.

Jan. 19th   Snow and more snow! This is Lynda's first time to see snow. "Oh, Mother," she said, "it's just pouring down—great big chips!"

Sister Buie kept the babies while I went to town to get my eyes tested and to buy Sharon some shoes.

I called off the other services and phoned Bug that we'd be home tomorrow.

Jan. 20th   Sharon was sick most of the night, so there was little rest for me. It was sleeting as the taxi took us to the train station. I witnessed to two ladies on the train who live in Port Arthur. Bug met us at the station. I left Marla with Sandra and went to vote. Dale is feeling fair—chicken pox has not hurt him much.

Jan. 21st   Bug got some more barrels, so I packed another one with used clothes, which makes eight. I let Dale stay out of bed for a while though he is still slightly speckled.

Jan. 22nd   My new glasses help—less headaches since I've had them. Plans call for me to be in Bossier City and Kilgore this coming Sunday.

Jan. 23rd   I wonder if I'm Jonah. I called off my East Texas trip because of ice and snow, and the bad weather has followed me home. Eight inches on the ground and a record low temperature—five above zero. The kids are fascinated, but I'm concerned about freezing water pipes. Our world is beautiful but *cold*!

Jan. 24th   I went to the laundry in De Ridder this morning. Later, Mittie Murphy came by to help me get off to Shreveport. I don't like leaving the other children, but I have no choice. I can bundle up Marla to keep her warm. I caught the first bus to leave going north since yesterday morning. Newspapers said "No snow in Shreveport." Reports were true.

Jan. 25th   I met Bug on January 25th —1937—my lucky day. I'll never forget how it was love at first sight. How I wish we were together today.

I taught Sister Doxie's Sunday school class and was impressed to preach from Matthew 25:23 in the morning service. Brother McDaniel asked me to stay for the evening service, but I had promised Brother Buie I'd be in Kilgore that night. So after dinner I took the bus. It was raining when I left and snowing when I arrived.

I felt like my sermon tonight was a miserable flop, but the gracious Lord baptized Leta Camp with the Holy Ghost. Her husband, who is Aubrey's Sunday school superintendent, serves as County Commissioner. There was much rejoicing tonight!

Jan. 26th   I can't shake this strong feeling that I'm needed at home. Aubrey and Gloria insist that I don't travel in this weather. Radio broadcasts say no improvement is expected soon, so I'll try to get the train tomorrow. I can be reasonably content away from my family if I'm busy for the Lord, but if not, I'm wretched.

Jan. 27th   The telephone line to Aubrey and Gloria's house is lying on the road. They took me to Longview to catch the train. It was due at 10:45, but it didn't arrive until 1:15, making me miss my connection in Shreveport. I stayed with Aubrey's mother until time to catch the 8:00 P.M. bus.

Jan. 28th   Arrived home shortly after midnight and immediately discovered why I was needed here. Bug and Sandra have the flu, and the cold front is moving south. I wanted to get Mittie Murphy to help us, but I couldn't get the car started. I walked into town to get some help and got a headache from the cold.

Jan. 29th   Nature's lavish hand has sheathed everything with a glistening crystal coat of ice—every blade of grass, every tiny twig and branch. I will forget, for a while, that power and telephone lines are down and that travel is interrupted. I will turn my attention from the bone-chilling cold and revel in this reckless display of silver beauty.

Jan. 30th   Bug's flu has made him miserable, but what a blessing Connie has been! The radio predicts sunshine tomorrow, so in spite of the ice, I went to the laundry today.

Jan. 31st   Chopped ice on a barrel of rain water to get needed water until we could get the water lines thawed. Broke ice off the clothes lines to hang wash.

Later, I packed another steel drum.

Feb. 1st   Bug was not able to go to church this morning. Good crowd in spite of the cold. Carl Ballestero's message on "His Name Shall be Called Wonderful," was excellent.

Feb. 2nd   This morning we went to Lake Charles to get some more barrels. Carl and Connie took me. Mama Wilkins heard we were coming and had gumbo fixed when we arrived. We hurried back home because Carl wanted to go to the fellowship meeting at Three Pine. I was able to stay home with my sick husband.

Feb. 3rd   Wash day again! I took Sister Murphy so she could do her washing too. I tried to work on an article Brother Glass has asked me to write for the De Ridder paper, but I couldn't seem to concentrate. I ended up working on it while housecleaning.

Feb. 4th   Mrs. Moses agreed to help me a day in exchange for some clothing. I am asking God to save her. Bug is much better.

Feb. 5th — Many visitors today—Brothers Wise, Dees, J.W. Magee, Lonnie Treadway, and Jimmy Miller among others. Bug left at 5:00 P.M. for a few days' tour in Mississippi. He will be in Booneville, Corinth, and Tupelo. Bless his heart, he wasn't really able to go, but God is able to bless him with strength and to make him a blessing.

Feb. 6th — The Pardues (called to China) came by for a visit. Marla cried almost all night, finally going to sleep at 5:00 A.M., but the Lord has wonderfully strengthened me.

My life is a rush of things all clamoring to get done at once. But through it all, "Jesus is my strength!"

Feb. 7th — The note at the bank had to be paid, so I made a hurried trip into town. Sandra's first day out of bed, and she made biscuits for breakfast. That child is such a help to me.

A letter from Brother Hopkins says he has failed to confirm our passage for this month or next. Our only hope is a cancellation. God is able!

Feb. 8th — I was so weary I overslept. Cold rain hindered Sunday school attendance. The baby was the only one I could take to service. Sandra has suffered a relapse with the flu.

Feb. 9th — It took all the money I could scrape together to pay for the washing and the telephone bill.

God bless Mittie Murphy for staying with the children. All of them are cross and irritable tonight. It's freezing outside, and I'm having to dry clothes by the fire.

Feb. 10th Two out, two down, and one to go. Now Lynda and Sharon have broken out with chicken pox. Only Marla still to take them.

Feb. 11th Marla has broken out. It's nice to know one always has the privilege of looking up!

Feb. 12th Still raining—not much sleep last night. Sharon is a sick little girl, and Marla is getting very speckled. Thank the Lord, Dale was able to go to school today.

Feb. 13th Marla is a pitiful little Job—chicken pox eruptions even on her eyelids and between her fingers. Sharon cried all night long. Vanna came over and prayed for the children. Oh, for just one night's sleep! I sent Bug a wire.

Feb. 14th Lovely sunshine! Thank God for some rest last night. I have felt so troubled in my spirit and have prayed all day.

Feb. 15th Sister Nash kept the children so I could go to Sunday school. Sandra stayed with them while I preached in morning worship. The Lord, in His mercy, blessed us. Bug arrived at 2:00. I felt bad that I didn't phone him that we were better, but it is wonderful having him with us. The service tonight proved that the Lord is in our midst. I know Romans 8:28 is valid in spite of these afflictions.

Feb. 16th   Homer will take Bug and Lawrence to Baton
             Rouge for the conference. Seems like he has
             barely come home, but I don't really mind. I
             hope the baby improves so I can attend one
             service—maybe Thursday.

Feb. 17th   Both Lucille and Mary helped today with my
             everlasting laundry problem. While I hung up
             and took down clothes, they folded and
             ironed.

Feb. 18th   Service last night was stiff, but praise the Lord,
             the sick and afflicted are improving.

Feb. 19th   Mary offered to clean house and watch the
             children if I would sew a dress for her. When I
             finished the dress, I did some mending—the
             first time in two weeks I've had a chance to
             sew.

Feb. 20th   Started the day with prayer, and so much was
             accomplished. Bug came home. He rode over
             with Brothers Evans and Glass to take an of-
             fering of $50 and some flowers to Brother
             Hayes, who has suffered a stroke. That dear,
             old man has been such an inspiration to all of
             us.

Feb. 21st   I placed my hands on those packed barrels
             today and asked the Lord to please move them
             to Africa—and us with them. The burden has
             never been greater.

             Brother Bennett called and wants me to start a
             meeting with him on Sunday night. The Kraus

sisters were scheduled but are having such a good meeting in De Ridder they hated to close out. I don't see how I can possibly hold a revival now. I'll just go for Sunday night.

Feb. 22nd   After going to see Mrs. Moses, who is in a pitiful condition, I barely had time to make it to De Quincy. Good crowd in spite of the cold. There was a tremendous altar service with a Catholic lady among the new seekers. After saying "No!" several different ways, I finally consented to return for a brief meeting.

Feb. 23rd   Yesterday morning after Sunday school, Bonnie, Vanna, and I held hands and agreed that God will open our way to Africa soon. We felt the witness of the Spirit. This is fellowship meeting night, so I don't have to go to De Quincy.

Feb. 24th   The weather is still miserable, so Bug will keep all the children except Marla Beth. I can bundle her up against the cold. Clothes dryers installed at the laundry are a great help. Bug took the baby and me to the train in De Ridder. We barely made it.

Feb. 25th   Good rest last night.

*   *   *   *

"I don't understand," queried my hostess as she leaned forward with her elbows on the table and gave me a look of deep contemplation.

"I've heard for years that the Freemans are going to Africa as missionaries, but . . . ," she paused, searching for tactful words to voice her questions.

"Do you *really* believe you'll ever go? Many of us are wondering. Don't misunderstand me—we're glad to have you preach for us, but if God has called you to Africa, what are you doing in De Quincy, Louisiana? Why is it taking so long to get off if it's God's will that you go? I hope you don't mind my asking, but I really would appreciate an explanation."

"Yes, it *has* been a long time. No, I don't mind your asking. And I'm not sure that I understand all of it, but I'll tell you the whole story if you have time to listen."

I paused, trying to decide on a starting place. She glanced at my baby in the basket and leaned back in her chair.

"Your baby is sleeping soundly, I have the whole afternoon, and I'm all ears."

The years melted as I went back.

2

Mr. and Mrs. Bug

Bug and I met as backsliders, both of us running from the same things—a call to preach and a call to go to Africa as a missionary. We found the Lord again (rather, He found us) just before we married in 1937, but we kept our secrets.

Bug didn't have the Holy Ghost when we married, but he prayed for it everywhere we went—Arkansas, Louisiana, Texas, and eventually New Mexico. All this time he was trying to persuade the Lord to give him the Spirit without his being willing to obey God's call.

Bug was an accountant for a wholesale grocery company. We lived in a small apartment nearby. Often we would weep and pray through his lunch hour. The nearest he came to sharing his burden with me was the day he said, "I'm troubled about all those black men who work in the warehouse who don't know the Lord."

That was true, but it wasn't the whole truth. Africa was calling him! Since he was seven or eight years old, he had known that he must go one day. Often he would wake his mother in the middle of the night, sobbing as though his heart were broken. But he would never answer when she asked, "What's wrong, Bug?" Motherlike, she would insist until he gave her a reason.

Usually, the only thing he could think of was, "My stomach hurts," or "I have an earache." Then she would bring out the castor oil or the ear drops.

Africa cost Bug many sleepless nights and unpleasant doses before he learned to conceal his feelings. When he grew older, he drifted from the Lord, always trying to shove his burden away. When I came into his life and we started praying together, the burden became a compelling force, demanding an answer. He was afraid. He feared losing me, and the unknown, unpredictable future that loomed before him was a cause of constant torment.

I sat in the front porch swing on a warm fall afternoon, embroidering a tablecloth and chatting with Mrs. Lucky, our landlady. She was called away, and I was left alone. Suddenly, the lazy daisies in my embroidery hoop changed into a lone, brown face with dark, searching eyes. It spoke to me.

"I am hungry! Will you bring me the Bread of Life?" I threw the cloth down and in agitation rushed down the steps.

The roses beside the path were pleading white faces. "Come and help us! You have the Light, and we wander in darkness!"

I hurried to the sidewalk in a desperate attempt to run away, but the hedges and the tree branches were full of faces—black, brown, white—all calling to me—a chorus of heartrending voices.

"Feed us, or we will die!"

"Bring us God's Word!"

"We thirst for the Water of Life!"

"Come . . . help us . . . we are waiting for you!"

I could move no further; tears rained from my eyes. I don't know how long I stood there paralyzed by the vision. Then it was gone.

Bug didn't notice my red eyes when he came home from work, but that was the evening he spoke of the "black men," and I nearly told my secret.

I received the Holy Spirit in Durham, Oklahoma, when I was eleven. That night I preached in the Spirit for two hours—to people of various races—Blacks, Asiatics, Indians, brown people, and white. I was terrified, thinking this to mean I would be called to so many different countries—Asia and Africa were evident, and I thought the brown people were natives of the South Sea Islands and the whites represented either Australia or New Zealand.

Following that, haunting dreams and visions often came to me, but I was hurrying away from the Lord then, so I would shake off their influence. Now, trying to draw nearer to Him, I was deeply moved. Still, I hid these things in my heart.

Ambitious plans for Bug's business career resulted in a transfer to Bastrop, Louisiana. Momentous events would occur there in just a few short months. Our first baby, Sandra, was born, and Ritchie Grocery Company, Bug's employer, burned to the ground. In subsequent events, we lost everything we had, except the baby.

After the fire, Bug was loaned temporarily to the insurance liquidators, and by a freak misunderstanding, he was the only one without a job when the staff was relocated. We owed less than a hundred dollars on our car and furniture, but when Bug could find neither money nor job, everything was repossessed.

Mr. and Mrs. Bug

My folks sent us train fare to New Mexico, and Dad offered Bug a job running a little grocery store he owned in Portales. The store was sold the day we arrived, so the ex-accountant began looking for odd jobs—anything to provide for his wife and baby daughter.

Soon after our arrival, Mother asked me to attend a Fellowship Day in her place. She was ill. As I passed her bed, she caught my hand: "Sister girl, when are you going to obey the Lord and acknowledge your call?"

She knew! Deeply disturbed, I mumbled something about Bug not having the Holy Ghost yet and hurried away. When I reached the place, something held me in the car. There was a compelling sense telling me that a vital decision must be made—NOW!

I put my head on the steering wheel and prayed. "Lord, I'm going into this service among strangers. Not one soul knows me here. If it is time for me to begin preaching, let someone here think I am a preacher. Amen."

My heart felt lighter . . . until I got to the entrance steps. A grubby, freckled-faced, little boy with red hair planted himself in front of me, put his hands in his pockets, looked up with an audacious grin, and said, "I'll bet you're a preacher!"

"Oh, no! This can't count—he's just a child!"

I managed a weak smile—"You'd lose your bet."

Inside, I sat down next to a friendly looking woman. She put her arm around me and whispered loudly, "I hope you're preaching today, dear."

"But . . . I . . . I'm not a preacher," I stammered.

She patted my shoulder. "I know—God does the preaching through you."

Shaken, I answered, "Excuse me," and retreated to the other side of the building.

This time I carefully chose an empty bench. No sooner had I sat down, however, than an elderly man on the seat in front of me, with white hair and a saintly face, turned around smiling and said, "God bless our preacher girls! Give us a good message today!"

I bolted for the car.

When I finally got home after a long, lonely drive, one matter was settled. I made my first attempt at preaching later that week.

The following Sunday we visited the Clovis church but had to leave service early since Bug's new job as a Pepsi Cola delivery man started at 4:00 A.M. In the earlier part of the service, however, without any show of emotion, Bug had lifted his heart to the Lord and said, "I surrender, Jesus. By Your grace, I will preach the gospel."

Monday night we came home as Mother was having evening prayers with my brothers. I tiptoed in and knelt with them. I heard a peculiar sound and opened my eyes. There sat Bug, cross-legged, with a rapt expression on his face, calmly speaking in other tongues and gesturing with his hands.

Our next move is *not* recommended for young preachers. They really *should* get some experience in a home church before they launch out.

3

Bug, Nona, and the Ministry

Ollie Davis lived in Corona, New Mexico, a little, western town isolated by majestic, rugged mountains, which helped it retain the "old west" atmosphere. She had long pled for workers to come hold services there. Bug decided this would be a good starting place for us, so he quit his job and we went. I was one sermon ahead of him. He preached his first one at Corona—in a street service held in front of a saloon. The audience was mostly cowboys with a pistol on one hip and a pint on the other.

We spent the days witnessing from house to house and held nightly services in the Davis's home, a beautiful old house built of massive, native rock slabs. One afternoon I passed a little, Mexican church and stopped to talk to the women who were cleaning inside and out. They said their priest only came once a year, and their hearts were hungry. They asked if I would please play "Ave Maria" on their little pump organ. I played it, then asked if they would like to learn some new songs. Soon we were singing joyously "Blessed be the Name," "There's Power in the Blood," and "When I Think of the Goodness of Jesus."

Long rays of the late afternoon sun finally reminded me that Bernice Davis was keeping my baby, who would need her bath before church time. I left the cleaning ladies reluctantly.

Prayer for thirty or forty minutes before service was a nightly ritual. That night, while everyone else prayed, I rocked Sandra to sleep in an old-fashioned chair with narrow slats in the back. I noticed, as I rocked, that it was past time for church to start and thought it strange that no one came. Then I heard a distinctive command. "Move!"

I glanced around. The eight others in the room were still talking to the Lord. I thought I must have imagined hearing a voice. But as I rocked back against the deeply set window behind me, the word came again, more urgently this time. "MOVE!" Thoroughly puzzled, I looked again. The scene was unchanged. While I wondered what it meant, I heard, as a shouted command, "GET UP AND MOVE!" I jumped out of the chair and went to Sister Davis, telling her what happened.

She closed the heavy drapes over the window without stepping in front of it. We couldn't understand why no one came for service but decided to have an all-night prayer meeting. That unforgettable night climaxed with foot washing at sunrise. Sister Davis gave a message in tongues and interpreted it:

To the darkest land of Africa you will go. You will wade through blood and water and suffer like Paul of old, but signs and wonders will be done in the name of Jesus, and there will be a great harvest of souls.

Bug, Nona, and the Ministry

I was kneeling across the room from Bug. When the Spirit lifted, Sister Davis looked around in amazement. "Who in this room is going to Africa?"

There was a sudden lilt of gladness in my heart. I had been so afraid to tell Bug about my call, but now fear was dissolved by a precious knowledge. When God told on us, we knew instantly without a word of discussion . . . *both of us were called to Africa!*

We looked at each other with sudden understanding and said simultaneously, "We are!"

A few minutes later a neighbor from across the street rushed in. "Thank God! You are all alive this morning. The Mexican women told their families about you singing with them yesterday afternoon, Nona. A fanatic young man got very drunk and came to kill you for desecrating their church. He was on the window ledge with a knife while you were rocking your baby. Every time you rocked, he lifted his knife to hurl it in your back. I kept praying, 'O God, make her move.' And finally you did! He brandished his knife and chased away the people who tried to come to church, too."

So that was why no one came!

We decided to keep our promise to visit a lonely, young lady herding sheep in the mountains. Her mother was dead and her stern father was thoughtless of her welfare. A friend of the Davis family loaned us a Model A Ford, but there was still quite a walk after we drove as far as we thought the car could safely go. We enjoyed a picnic lunch against the pleasant background of God's ancient rock sculpture, dwarf pines, and jagged peaks. The girl's dun pony grazed nearby with dropped reins.

"Is your horse gentle?" Bug asked.

"Amiable as a friendly dog," she answered. Bug mounted and rode around awhile.

When he came back, he asked, "Will he ride double?"

"Oh, yes, my brother and I rode him double to school."

"Come, Nona," Bug said. "You have on a wide skirt; climb on with me."

With that, he moved behind the saddle and helped me in it. I was barely on when the mountain pony became a malevolent bundle of bucking, plunging fury. Bug watched for a safe chance and slid off, hoping the horse would calm down with one less rider. He didn't. I concentrated on hanging on and did not hear Bug shouting, "Jump off! Jump off!" The horse ran bucking, twisting, and snorting with such incredible speed the shouting pursuers were left far behind. With malicious cunning, he ran for some low-limbed trees and used them to rake me off. It was fortunate that I fell doubled up so that my arms and legs caught the brunt of his vicious attack. He kicked and pawed me with flying hooves until Bug and the others caught up with us. We soon discovered I was completely numb from the waist down, with acute pain in my back.

They made me as comfortable as possible under the tree and went to hunt a passable road around the mountain. Model As were sturdy and could rough it, so they finally reached where I lay. Back at the Davis's home, we had to decide what next. The nearest doctor was 75 miles, the nearest hospital 150 miles, and we had neither transport nor money. Bug asked, "What do you think we should do?"

"There's only one thing left . . . trust the Lord."

The following day, my feet and legs were still lifeless. Bernice stayed with me while everyone else went to the street service. I awoke from a nap with the thought, "Faith does not lie passive; it acts!" I called Bernice.

"Put my slippers on my feet, please, and turn me around on the bed so my feet are on the floor."

"O.K.," she said. "Now what?"

"You take my hands and pull me up while we both say together, 'In the name of Jesus.'" She pulled, and as the weight came on my legs, I thought I was going to fall. But instead, it felt like an electric shock hit my back, and life came back into my limbs. I started screaming, and Bernice was a little disgusted.

"The Lord has healed your back. Now what's wrong?"

"The feeling has come back to all the bruises and the places where about a square yard of skin is missing. But, praise God, I feel it!"

Bug was at the gate when he heard me scream. He came running. "What's wrong?"

"Not wrong, dear, RIGHT! God has healed me."

We left Corona with one goal—Africa. Most of our friends were skeptical. There were only two who encouraged us, Dale Struble, pastor in Albuquerque, and my mother.

4

Four Rounds with the Missionary Board

Mother loaned us her car that fall (1939) to go to East St. Louis, Illinois, to meet the Missionary Board.

Our youth and inexperience were evident. There was not a lot of finesse with those conscientious leaders. We stood as prisoners at the bar while they discussed our merits and otherwise. "Otherwise" tipped the scale.

One said, "You both look rather delicate. (I weighed 108 pounds, Bug 125, and we are both *tall*!) Haven't you made a mistake? Maybe it's the TB asylum you need."

Another commented, "I don't know this young man. He may make it, but I've known this girl most of her life and she is definitely not missionary material . . . too high strung and temperamental."

But their conclusion was solid wisdom. Harry Morse summed it up. "Go work, preach, evangelize, pastor, build a church or two. Don't trade on a call to Africa; don't even mention it. But if you still feel called, come back in three years."

We helped Mother revive the work at Portales, built a church, and later pastored there. We went to the Rio

Grande valley and made a good start on opening a work in Harlingen. We decided our circumstances were intolerable and left. Like Jonah, we were swallowed by a whale of trouble.

Our only son, Dale, was born prematurely when I had pneumonia. Both of our lives hung in the balance for five days before the Lord healed us.

We moved to De Ridder where Bug worked at Camp Polk to pay the hospital bill. We accepted the pastorate of the church at Rosepine in April 1941 and requested to meet the Missionary Board at the fall conference in Houston the same year. They asked us to wait another year.

Our daughter, Lynda, was born in October of 1942, so I missed the conference in Jackson, Tennessee.

We thought we would get our missionary appointment in 1943. After we waited the whole afternoon, the Board came out of a closed session just as it was time for the night service to begin and said, "Sorry, we don't have time to talk to you this conference; come back next year."

We went home, and the two of us had still another all-night prayer meeting. In the early hours of the morning, God gave us a scripture in such a beautiful way. It will surely be our anchor as long as we live.

> *Ye have not chosen me, but I have chosen you, and ordained you, that ye should GO and bring forth fruit, and that your fruit should remain: that whatsoever ye shall ask of the Father in my name, he may give it you.*
>
> *(John 15:16)*

At sunrise we held each other's hands and settled for all time that, by God's grace, Africa was still our goal. We would GO no matter how many "next years" intervened.

Louisiana and East Texas were then counted as one district. The district conference held early in '44 was at Port Arthur. George Glass was host pastor. My brother, Johnny, who was in the Navy, had a few days' leave from his ship. He phoned me from Farwell, Texas, where Mother was living.

"Mother is very sick, Sis, and I want to see you so badly. Can you come?"

I told him about the conference and promised to phone him from Port Arthur. Bug left it up to me, so I packed and planned to leave by train for West Texas after a day of services.

When A. O. Moore, our missionary secretary, heard my plans, he said, "I wish you would stay for the whole conference. I can't make a promise, and I have no grounds for feeling as I do, but something may be said about Africa. You would need to be here."

I phoned Johnny and told him I couldn't come.

He begged, "Sis, Mother is so very sick. She needs you. If you leave there today, we'll only have one day together before I have to go. Sis, I already know I'm not coming back from this war . . . this could be your last chance to see me."

I promised to pray and to let him know in an hour. It was a bitter hour of temptation. Mother needed me, and I desperately wanted to see a beloved brother. There was no clear answer to my prayer maybe because I prayed with a divided heart. Then there was a still, small voice,

He that loveth father or mother more than me is not worthy of me (Matthew 10:37).

and ". . . something may be said about Africa."

"Sorry, Johnny—I wanted so much to come, but Jesus has to be first. . . ."

On the last afternoon of the conference, the District Board gave Brother Moore time to speak about missions. He began by saying that he wanted to introduce a young couple with a burden for Africa and called us to the platform. There was a gasp from the audience. Members of our church in Rosepine were shocked, and many of our friends were astonished, for we had obeyed instructions and spoke to no one but Jesus. Neither of us were able to speak; we simply stood and wept. Brother Glass moved forward: "The Freemans are our friends. We love them and do not want them to leave our district, but if God has called them to Africa, we'd better help them go."

With that, he opened a guitar case and set it on the altar, and a spirit of giving swept the audience. It reached even to the outside. People about to get in their cars to leave felt a sudden impulse to return and *give*. Everyone wept with us, and some made two or three trips to the guitar case. One lady, her first time by, said, "That's my new shoes," as she put in several dollar bills. The next time, more dollars—"That's my new dress." On her final trip, she emptied her billfold—"There goes my new coat, hallelujah!"

The love offering totaled $3,300.00. Several weeks later, when the Missionary Board met again, we were notified of our appointment to Africa. Because of the war, there was no hope of immediate departure, so we were asked to travel as much as possible in the interest of missions. We did—extensively.

Quite unexpectedly, while we were in the Northwest

raising money for India, the Lord arranged for Johnny and me to have three precious days together. A memory to forever cherish. He went down with his ship six months later.

5

To Africa—At Last!

World War II finally ground to a halt, and we made application to the Belgian Congo. The Lord had not spoken to us of a specific country in Africa. We decided, after much prayer, that the middle of the continent would be an appropriate beginning. But that door did not open. We moved down on the map to Broken Hill, Northern Rhodesia, and received enough encouragement to start packing drums of equipment. Then we were asked to supply the last requirement—a letter of guarantee from a property owner there. Both Northern and Southern Rhodesia closed to us because we lacked contacts, but miraculously, the door opened to South Africa. We filled out stacks of application papers (requiring sixty-nine notary seals), sent them off, and eventually the good news came—we were accepted! It was late 1946.

Do you remember the camp meeting in De Quincy that year? Johnny Thomas reminded the folks that we were soon going to Africa. When he asked how many would pray for us, many hands lifted in promise. "Now," he said, "you've heard of putting *legs* on your prayers? Well, we want you to put wheels on these. We are going to buy the Freemans a car to use in Africa." The money was raised in a matter of minutes.

We thought, *now* we will go! Sharon, our third daughter, had been born in '45 while we wrestled with visa applications. We thought she would be our last baby, but early in '47, we learned she wasn't! So we waited for Marla to make her appearance—in August.

Then we hit another snag. The whole world seemed to be traveling since the war was over. Elmo Hopkins of Indianapolis, a man experienced in such matters, tried every travel agency in the book. There were just no reservations available for a family of seven. "They say it could be *two more years* before you are able to go."

* * * *

"Sister Rosa, the road we have traveled *has* been long, and I've only hit the high spots in relating it to you, but let me say how I feel. All of these things have happened to get us ready. We haven't gone because it wasn't God's time for us to go. But when God's appointed time comes, doors will open and everything will fall into place like the last few pieces of a jigsaw puzzle."

I clapped my hands for emphasis; and at that exact moment, someone knocked on the door: "Long distance telephone call for Sister Freeman at the grocery store."

"I'll watch the baby," Rosa said. "Go on and take your call."

It was Bug. He asked casually, "Could we leave for Africa next Tuesday?"

"We could leave tomorrow the way I feel," I answered. "But are you serious?" He was. "There is an opening on the *Genevieve Lykes* if we can get ready in a hurry."

"Just tell me what to do."

"See if Brother Bennett will take you to Lake Charles to look for a steamer trunk. Close out the meeting tonight, and ask them to bring you home after service. I'll phone Mama to see if she and Tula (his oldest sister) can come lend a hand. The Lord will help us, and we'll make it."

I breathed a fervent "Amen!" and hurried back to Rosa and my baby. When I dashed in the door, I told her.

"After I gave you that long history, I said 'God will open doors in His time!' Well, He has! This is IT! We leave for Africa next week!"

That was a busy afternoon. We found the trunk and a fiber drum for packing at Lake Charles. Service that night was unusual; some were filled with the Holy Ghost and I felt like I was only touching the ground in high spots.

* * * *

Feb. 26th   I failed to get enough barrels in Lake Charles, but the Lord provided. The man from the Coca-Cola plant phoned to say he had three we could have. I sent for Annie—she knows more about packing used clothing than anyone. I sent most of the quilts and blankets to the laundry to be washed and dried. We're drying clothes by the fire and with the iron.

Sister Johnson fixed dinner for all the helpers. Everyone is being so kind. Letty kept Lynda and Sharon for me and made buttonholes in some dresses and shirts.

I phoned Mother and Grandmother with the big news. Bug was trying to phone Brother Stairs—finally caught up with him at a train station somewhere between St. Louis and Canada. I've written as many cards as possible—inviting our friends to the farewell service at the church on Monday night, March 1st. Granny, Tula, and Sug (Bug's mother and two sisters) arrived by train with Bonnie, Bug's nephew. I called Bonnie to tell her how quickly the Lord had answered our agreement in His name.

Feb. 27th   Granny is such a help with Sharon and Marla. Sug and Tula take turns at the sewing machine, and Bonnie is a handy errand runner.

Sister Johnson fixed dinner for us again today. I learned that if I climbed in the barrels and jumped up and down, I could get more in them. I was able to condense eleven barrels of clothing into nine by doing this.

Bug and I are weary but so happy. It almost seems like a dream!

Feb. 28th   Lynda and Sandra spent the night in De Quincy with Esther Pharis. I'm worried about Lynda—still feverish. Hollie Lee traded Bug a good watch for his old one. It looks nice.

Brother Wilkins phoned and wanted me to preach for them in Lake Charles tonight. I was so weary—not much of a sermon I fear. "Pop" Wilkins and Evelyn brought me home after service.

Feb. 29th   The loose ends that had dangled for months are now knitting together so perfectly that at times I feel like a mere spectator.

We had a Sunday school contest, and Bug's side lost and had to feed my side. This was the Lord's way of arranging a marvelous church dinner for our last Sunday in Rosepine. Our cooks went overboard with huge baskets lavishly loaded with delicious food—enough to feed a small army.

I phoned Daddy to say good-bye. Clara and Grandmother phoned me.

Arthur Lewis came for the barrels and crates early this morning. I can't describe my feelings as I saw them leave.

Bug has been worried about his "one man" Catahoula hog dog. We've tried giving him away on several occasions, but we had to bring him home each time. Several people wanted to buy him, but we knew that wouldn't work either. But as the truck with our freight left, he stood by the side of the road and watched until they were out of sight. Then he moved to the middle of the road and stood there like a soldier at his post. A few minutes later, he was hit by a car. Merciful death came instantly. It seemed deliberate, for Alexander had grown up beside busy Highway 171. We were all saddened but realized he had solved our problem in his own way.

Mar. 1st   Final washing! Paid bills and took care of some last minute odds and ends.

Tonight's service will be a precious memory for as long as I live. The church was packed in spite of the cold rain. George Glass was the master of ceremonies. Among the preachers present were Brothers Wise, Clanton, Johnson, Self, Wilkins, Laidlow, Pardue, Sylvester, Sonenburg, Norsworthy, and Laurent. It was a little like attending one's own funeral when we stood at the front and everyone came by to greet us as the congregation sang, "God Be With You Till We Meet Again."

After service we were driven to the train station in De Quincy, where Brother Bennett and many in his congregation were waiting to see us off. There were final sad, yet sweet, farewells, and the train pulled out of the station a little after 1:00 A.M. We are due to arrive in New Orleans at 7:20 A.M.

Mar. 2nd   After boarding, I put the baby in her buggy and made Sandra and Lynda as comfortable as possible in the lounge. All of us slept some. Lynda is still sick—coughing a lot.

Johnny Thomas met us at the depot and took

us to his home, where his wife made delicious waffles for breakfast.

Someone threw a brick through the car window, evidently planning to take our suitcases, but Bug and Johnny returned too quickly, and the thief ran away.

Our boat is scheduled to sail tomorrow, but it is fogbound at the mouth of the Mississippi. It will first have to dock and be loaded.

Because of bad weather, we didn't take the children to church with us tonight. It was nice to see our old friends in New Orleans.

Mar. 3rd   Aline kept the children today while Bug and I did some shopping for clothes.

Very good service tonight! Our friends are going to provide mail for us on the long trip. Upon departing, we'll be given a bundle of letters with a date for the opening of each envelope.

Mar. 4th   The Lykes Line agent notified Bug that the senior man at the Maritime Control Office wanted to see him. Bug walked into his office and said:

"I'm Reverend Freeman. I believe you wanted to see me."

"Yes," the man answered. "I wanted to meet the man we waived the rule for. It is against regulations for a cargo vessel to carry more than twelve passengers without a medical doctor on board. Your baby makes a total of thirteen passengers, but we've decided you can go anyway. Possibly the boat will sail tomorrow."

Mar. 5th   Rain! Rain! Rain! The boat could not load its cargo, so we're still waiting. There are reports of violent storms in the gulf. One ship is aground in the mouth of the river. The street in front of the Thomas' house has become a river. Dale has shared none of our apprehensions about the delayed departure, thoroughly enjoying himself as he helped the neighborhood boys deliver groceries in a canoe.

Johnny Thomas did *not* share Dale's enthusiasm for the rising water. When it was but an inch or so from flooding the interior of his new car, he asked, "Bug, can't we pray about this?"

Bug agreed, and together they rebuked the floodwaters in the name of Jesus. Bug's fervor could have been encouraged by another motive, but nevertheless, within an hour the water had receded an inch or so, and by midnight the pavement was once again visible.

This is the first day I can say that Lynda is better. Then, the little darling climbed on the clothes hamper in the bathroom, fell, and skinned her back. We have a lot of sore arms from smallpox vaccinations. Sandra and Sharon have fevers from it.

Mar. 6th   Rain finally stopped in the night, and the water is slowly receding. Brother and Sister Thomas have been so good to us and the hospitality gracious in spite of seven of us crowding in on them. I'm anxious to stop imposing and get going, but,

"Lord, Thy will be done."

A ray of light! A call from the office late this afternoon instructed us to be on board at 11:30 tomorrow morning. The proposed sailing time is 12:00 noon. Sounds wonderful—I hope this is the end of postponements.

Mar. 7th   I can hardly believe this day is a reality!

Bug had to make two taxi trips to get all our luggage on the boat. Later, he met us at church for Sunday school. They checked the roll, allowed us to make short talks, then dismissed everyone to go see us off. Just as we reached the wharf, two taxis brought the Udd family, our fellow travelers, who are Assemblies of God missionaries to Nyasaland. How wonderful of the Lord to provide us congenial companions for the trip.

All the folks came on board to see the spacious, well-furnished cabins on the *SS Genevieve Lykes*. After they left, we stood on the deck, holding the ends of ribbons that we threw to those seeing us off. Aline played the accordion and Johnny his horn as the boat moved slowly from the wharf. The ribbons broke as they sang, "When I Think of the Goodness of Jesus." Then, Johnny played "Farewell to Thee." The sweet sound grew fainter and fainter, and soon our friends looked like a cluster of small, doll-like figures silhouetted against the somber warehouse background. As the sounds of the music died in the distance, I felt the first pangs of parting. But, we are on our way to Africa, at last, and this is happiness edged with the sadness of good-bye. Both of us feel a deep assurance that we are moving in the will of God.

Mar. 8th The passenger list of thirteen includes seven Freemans, five Udds, and an elderly German woman who emigrated to the States several years ago. The climate here did not agree with her, so she is returning to West Africa. Her accent is so thick that I can barely understand her.

6
Bug's Crew Afloat

Mar. 9th   We have finally left the muddy Mississippi and are now sailing in the Gulf of Mexico. On our way out, we passed the ship that had been grounded at the mouth of the river. I didn't expect such vivid blue seas or the sailing to be so smooth. We passed the Florida Keys on our left. The captain pointed out an old fort where a man named Smith, one of the conspirators in Lincoln's assassination, was held.

Mar. 10th   We passed Cuba this morning, saw a number of sailboats off the coast.

Today, I used the ship's washing machine for the first time. The mate had two ropes stretched on the top deck. It was quite a hassle to get the wet clothes hung up in the brisk wind—using straight and safety pins. My arms and face are blistered.

The Udds are very pleasant traveling companions. They spent three years in the Congo, but after she contracted blackwater fever (a type of malaria) they moved to Nyasaland.

Mar. 11th The color scheme for today is blue trimmed with white. The wind is rising, and though the white caps on each wave are lovely, their effect on my stomach is not so good.

Oh dear, I am forced to conclude that my three youngest have whooping cough. There is one consolation—I have plenty of time to care for them.

Mar. 12th We are between the Caribbean and the Atlantic, and the sailing is rough. News from home of a terrible blizzard raging, and here we sit on deck with a pleasant breeze and clear sunshine, watching the azure water ever moving in liquid blue hills and valleys. The captain brought out some deck chairs that are very comfortable.

Sandra "lost" her breakfast this morning. None of us have been *really* sick except my three "whoopers," and their conditions seem to vary from hour to hour.

Mar. 13th I went down in the hold to help Sister Udd wash, but the motion of the boat and the swish of the washing machine made me so dizzy I had to desert her.

The captain showed us our course on the

map. We are due in Cape Town on March 29th. We saw the shadowy, mountainous outline of the Island of Martinique this afternoon and its lights tonight. This will be our last sight of land for the next two weeks. Rough sea now.

Mar. 14th   We had Sunday school for the children in the Udd's cabin this morning. They have a "Scripture match" in our cabin every night.

Sister Udd is sick—a bout with malaria. I'm afraid the washing didn't help. Marla is coughing badly, but Sharon is better.

Mar. 15th   Wash day again! What a wrestling match—trying to hang out wet clothes in a gale. Marla has fever—coughed and cried most of the night.

Mar. 16th   Water! Water! Water! I wish I could read, but it makes me dizzy. I didn't realize I was so weary until I tried to relax. I must rest when my poor little coughers give me a chance.

Mar. 17th   My baby is so very sick. Thank God, I know Him and know that He is able to do anything my faith can reach Him for.

Mar. 18th   We crossed the equator at 6:00 P.M. The crew had fun teasing the children—telling them there would be a black line and a bump. The clouds hang so low that one has the sensation of being able to reach up and touch them.

Mar. 19th   It is difficult to sever old connections. I have carried a burden for Rosepine for seven years. So I suppose it's not strange that I felt it last night. As so often before, I visited each home in prayer.

Mar. 20th   I'm weary from another wind-wrestled washing. Marla slept better after prayer by Bug and Brother Udd.

Mar. 21st   We had a "sing-song" and "Scripture match" on deck this morning. I do miss services.

Mar. 22nd   Thank the Lord, the ironing is done. I prayed while I ironed, "Lord, smooth me into a better soul winner." I asked Bug and Brother Udd to pray for Marla again. She is such a sweet, playful baby between coughing spells. Lynda and Sharon are better.

Mar. 23rd   The children are getting bored with ship life. The captain says we should reach Cape Town next Monday.

I am earnestly praying for full "spiritual equipment" in our new field of labor.

My baby is still very sick.

Mar. 24th   We received a radiogram from the man we hope to work with in South Africa. His message was, "May millions be blessed through your immigration to our country."

The captain came by to see us today and thanked us for being a "lady and gentleman" on his boat. He also commended the behavior of our children and said to Bug, "You are the most pleasant, humorous reverend that has ever sailed with me!"

Mar. 25th   We are more than anxious for the journey's end. I started packing again today. Had it not been for the whooping cough, this would have been a pleasant vacation. Bug and I have both gained weight, but we are eager to get into the harness again.

Marla has improved slightly.

Mar. 26th   Less wind, so this was my most pleasant wash day. We have entered the Cape rollers. Great swells of water are rising and falling. This will continue for the rest of the trip.

The captain called me into his office today. He has cabled a doctor to meet the boat upon our arrival. If it's determined that Marla's cough is contagious, it will prove necessary to quarantine the entire ship for two weeks. He seemed really upset, which caused me to feel quite bad. I had a good prayer meeting, however, and my Jesus assured me that everything will be all right.

Mar. 27th   The rollers are still rolling! This is the roughest sea we have encountered thus far. Just when we had settled down for the night, there was a sudden lurching of the boat, quickly followed by a crash—my toilet article bag falling to the floor, breaking the mirror and two bottles.

While Sandra and I were cleaning the mess, the radio operator brought a message from Brother Goss, assuring us that we would be met at Cape Town.

Mar. 28th   Easter! How strange to be so far from all those we love, and worst of all, no Easter service. Just as we started to have our own little service, the captain called us into his cabin to listen to a church broadcast. It was so uninspired and dry that I decided that if that was all I knew of religion, I would probably be a skeptic like the captain claims he is.

I will rest well tonight since my apprehensions about the doctor's verdict are gone.

7

Come and See!

Mar. 29th About 10:00 A.M. Sister Udd came running to our porthole and exclaimed, "Come and see—land!" First, there was but a misty outline, then gradually, as we came nearer, Cape Town and the surrounding mountains came into view. We climbed to the top deck to take pictures and rejoiced that our Lord had brought us safely thus far.

Cape Town is lovely! Most of the roofs are red and the walls like a rich cream. We couldn't stop looking. As our boat nudged the dock, we spotted a huge sign which read, "Welcome to Reverend Freeman and Family."

When the doctor came on board, he glanced at Marla and said, "She may have had pneumonia, but she's well on the road to recovery now." He recommended that I fly with her to Pretoria and not risk the tedious thousand-mile journey by train.

Custom and immigration formalities did not take long, and after three weeks of water, we had the wonderful feel of solid ground under our feet again. Our new friends took us by taxi (actually two taxis) to the home where we would spend the night. The owners were away, so another family provided refreshments. When we left the boat, it was 4:30 in the afternoon and warm, but sunset brought chill winds. The quaint house where we are staying has a long hall with rooms opening off either side. Though I'm sure the architect didn't plan it as such, the effect is that of a wind tunnel nevertheless. Brrr! We are all cold, and there are no heaters.

Mar. 30th In our long talk last night, we were introduced to some history that is sacred to the Afrikaner—such as the murder of Piet Retief at Blood River and the subsequent victory and Covenant, which is remembered every December 16th.

The plane ticket for me (and the baby) will cost $64—far in excess of our budget. Marla coughed and cried so much last night that our friend called the doctor. He diagnosed her condition as bronchitis and insisted that I fly with her. The trains here are smaller than those in the U.S.—rough and drafty. How nice it would be if all of us could fly!

Bug arranged for our freight to go by rail. He has a compartment for him and the children on a train leaving at 10:00 P.M. It will take two full days for them to reach Pretoria. A lady we met packed a lunch for them—for five pounds. We will have to get accustomed to coarse, dark brown bread and limitless quantities of hot tea.

Our English is as strange to our new friends as theirs is to us.

My flight is scheduled for 7:30 tomorrow morning.

Mar. 31st I asked the Lord to help me wake up at 4:00 A.M.—which He did even though I had slept less than two hours. After a cup of tea, we walked five blocks to get a bus to town. Next, there was another long walk for the airport bus. Fog was so heavy the plane took off an hour late. This was my first time to fly, and I was a little fearful. Still, it was a thrilling sensation to climb steadily through the swirls of gray fog and milky clouds into the company of mountain peaks and bright sunshine.

Suddenly, as we were passing over the karoo (the dry tableland in South Africa), I was back in Lake Charles, Louisiana, in a very unusual service. A dear, old, French lady, who looked like an angel dressed in white, gave a message in tongues, then interpreted it in French. Brother Fuselier whispered the message to me in English:

When you find yourself flying over Africa with

your baby, this will be a sign to you that God has sent you to reap a great harvest of souls. You must not doubt nor be afraid, for the Lord is with you.

That night I was full of doubts and questions. Our youngest was no longer a baby, we didn't plan to fly, and why would I be traveling alone?

I returned to my present surroundings as the plane jolted with the impact of a sudden storm. In the ensuing minutes, many of the passengers became sick, so under cover of the confusion, I was able to have a private praise meeting with my Lord—thanking Him for His wonderful ways of guiding and directing His children.

We made two stops before finally landing at a temporary airport near Johannesburg. Brother Goss and the Beetges (father and son) met us there, and together we drove the fifty-six miles into Pretoria. There was some confusion as to where we were to stay, but eventually hospitality was offered at the Thompsons. A lady kept Marla for an hour while I attended the evening service and greeted the folks.

Apr. 1st This was a long day—waiting for the arrival of Bug and the children at 7:00 P.M. He had his problems on the long train ride. I hadn't thought of including soap with their toiletries, and none was available on the train. Every time the train stopped, Bug tried to buy soap, but they would not sell him a bar unless he bought $20.00 worth of groceries. He felt he was already burdened with too many bundles, suitcases, and children to wrestle with groceries, too. Soot and dust blew continually through the open windows, and by the second day, they were a grimy bunch, to say the least.

Just out of Pretoria, he tried to clean dirty faces, arms, and legs with a generous application of brushless shaving cream. This distributed the dirt in a more or less gray film. The appalling result contrasted sharply with their blue eyes and fair hair. When I saw them stepping off the train, I screamed, "My children have contracted some sort of African skin disease!" Bug grunted a decidedly unsympathetic, "Shut up!" Then later, he told me, "It's your fault—you didn't give us any soap." How thankful I was to see their usual rosy complexions emerge sometime later from the bathtub.

We hurried to church for my first experience at preaching with an interpreter. The lady did fine, but I hesitated too often and several times forgot my train of thought. I finally found enough liberty for the Lord to move in hearts, and several people came forward for prayer. Their ways are certainly different—only one or two preachers prayed with the seekers. Though many things seem strange to us, we are ever so grateful to be here.

Apr. 2nd   Today was "Ladies Day"—different! I spoke briefly in the evening service and felt more freedom. Brother Goss preached. We expected Brother Pair to arrive tomorrow, but he surprised us about 11:30 this evening. We talked well into the night.

Apr. 3rd   I missed the afternoon service to assist Brother Goss with a report for *The Pentecostal Herald.* We worked on it until quite late. A welcome service was planned for all of us tonight, and I was only half ready when a car came for our family. I didn't know what to do with Marla, but a young man, Pieter Grobler, who boards with the Thompsons, offered to keep her. The tent was beautifully decorated with the flags and colors of Canada, the United States, and South Africa. I had never seen such gorgeous flowers before. Just as refreshments were being served, a message arrived that Marla was crying and Pieter couldn't get her quiet, so I hurried home to her.

Apr. 4th   I stayed with the baby tonight while everyone else went to church. Bug went to a baptismal service this afternoon. There are conditions here that make me very heartsore, and I have wept and prayed most of the day.

Apr. 5th   The highlight of the day was meeting some African preachers with whom we will be working. One named Shai impressed us the most.

Apr. 6th We went today to register as immigrants. We must have eight pictures—four each—front and profile. Some friends took us for a drive; we saw grass-thatched, native mud huts. The children were entranced by teams of oxen, six and seven double, pulling wagons.

Apr. 9th Conference today with the brethren concerning our future. We only desire to be led of the Lord. Wearing a hat to every service is a decided burden for me, but I'll conform. I don't want to offend. I can't help but think the Lord would prefer less paint and more hair, regardless of hats.

Apr. 10th I've had to give Sofie, the native woman, five shillings more per week because our washing is so big. She washes on a flat board, and my clothes look horrible. Die, Pride!

Apr. 11th The government has closed all Sunday schools until further notice because of a polio epidemic. Bug preached this morning. The Paul Malans invited us for lunch. Their baby was ill with tonsillitis. There was a big crowd to start with tonight, but I preached to many as they were leaving—all during the service. Still, some were touched by the gospel.

Apr. 12th We are finally registered with Immigration (after three efforts). The cost was one pound per person except for the baby. We will have to file application for her later.

A family named Botha invited all the Americans for dinner. Delicious! It's been a long time since we've had a meal like that. When one of the daughters took us home, she slipped a pound into my hand. That was welcome, too.

Apr. 13th   Bug and Marla have the flu with high fever. Milk here is neither pasteurized nor delivered to your door. One has to go to the dairy with his own container, then bring the milk home and heat it to make it safe to drink.

This country is at least fifteen years behind the U.S. I think its progress was greatly hindered by the War. The music preferred in our neighborhood was canned in America some time ago, and we are subjected to loud blasts of it every evening. There are no door or window screens and definitely no central heating. I am continually amazed by the warm, pleasant days, followed by the cold, bone-chilling nights.

Apr. 14th   Our freight is here! We took the keys to the shipping agent today. I had to buy a pair of cheap scissors. Both of mine "disappeared," and my sewing thread seems to be "melting." I don't like the idea of locking everything up, but I'm beginning to understand why everyone around us does. My sick family is better, thank God!

Apr. 15th   Inactivity is making us restless. There are services every Sunday but not much in between. We have been busy full scale in the Lord's work for too long to be satisfied with this leisurely approach. Perhaps we need the vacation, but we have a deep desire to thrust out into the harvest.

Apr. 16th   We took the children to the zoo. It was Lynda's first time to go, and we enjoyed her excited reaction to the animals and birds.

Apr. 17th   We went into town today to check furniture prices, and my dream of some decent furniture quickly vanished! If and when we have means to buy, we will check the auction sales, which are held weekly.

Cold and rainy tonight. A Brother De Witt took us to Johannesburg for services. Brother Pair blessed me, singing "My Heavenly Father Watches Over Me." I needed the reassurance—we learned today that the Malan's baby has suspected polio and has been placed in the isolation ward at the hospital.

Apr. 18th   I am continually watching the African women. Years of carrying loads on their heads give them a certain gracefulness. One has just passed with a large pan of boiled corn on her head and a laughing six month old on her back. I want so much to communicate with them, but so few understand English. We are studying Afrikaans, but the guttural sounds are difficult for our southern American tongues.

Apr. 19th   Brother Goss left for Cape Town and home today.

There is a thornbush here whose name translated is "Wait a bit." It should be the national anthem. We must need to learn patience badly—everything moves so slowly.

"Lord, help me to be cheerful—living with continual frustration."

Apr. 20th   A letter from Anne lifted our burden for Rosepine. Willie Owens is the new pastor. My God doeth all things well!

Apr. 21st   A wearisome day, trying to clear our freight. There is a twelve hundred pound difference in the weight as charged by the boat and the railway. If we can get it adjusted, it will result in quite a savings. We went to several widely scattered offices, but none of them was the right one.

Apr. 22nd   We spent most of the day at the King's Warehouse. The customs officer was quite suspicious and very rude at first. We tried to stay patient and act courteous—gave him some *Heralds,* witnessed a little, and tried to do everything he requested. After a while, he changed his attitude and became very helpful. The used clothing will have to be fumigated next week, but he released everything else, and Uncle Hans Botes hauled it for us.

Come and See!

The Malan baby is much improved.

Apr. 23rd   The linens were musty from being packed so long, so I have aired everything and repacked it in my trunk in the house. The books and equipment will have to be stored in the garage. I'll be so happy when the Lord provides us a home, but I'll do my best to remain patient *until*!

Apr. 25th   My soul cries out for revival in the land. Tonight I preached from Acts 2:1-4, stressing Pentecost then and now. Some walked out, but many prayed with us at the close. If the Lord does not give us wisdom, I am sure we will utterly fail. But, oh, the need is so great!

Apr. 26th   The used clothing has been fumigated, brought home damp, hung up to be dried and repacked, and I am exhausted.

Our freight and customs charges were forty pounds, and we didn't have it, but a new friend, Brother Terblanche, loaned us the money. God is good! Our financial situation is precarious, but we are learning more about TRUST!

May 4th   We started 4:00 A.M. prayer meetings last week. Folks who are hungry for God come by and pray until time to leave for work or school. Great results! I don't know exactly how many have been filled with the Holy Spirit, but several every morning.

The customs officer and his mother came to church—his first time to attend a service in twenty years. He is an alcoholic—I do pray he will receive deliverance.

May 10th   The people are so stirred they have requested a week of special services. This is the fourth night. Bug preached a mighty message—revival fires are burning. Souls are being born of the Spirit in every service.

May 20th   We enjoyed the revival while it lasted, but wrangling and dissension are effective wet blankets. There are folks who walk out every time Bug or I step up to preach. We are having doubts about the workability of our situation.

May 28th   Bug is very ill. We have discovered he is allergic to coal smoke, especially when the fires are first made. Everyone here cooks on coal stoves. The area where we are living is low, and an unhealthy pall of foggy smoke hangs over us every morning until the sun dispels it about 10:00 or 11:00. Then, about 3:30 or 4:00 in the afternoon, it begins creeping back. The house is so cold. There are twelve of us and only one ancient bathroom.

June 5th   Bug felt like walking to the post office this morning—no mail as usual. Sometimes the days seem terribly long and tedious. We are penniless! Evidently, we need to be in that

Come and See!

condition, for the Lord promised to supply our needs. I'm certainly glad the Book says:

"He knoweth the way that I take: when he hath tried me, I shall come forth as gold."

I hope I never again take decent home life and nutrition for granted. I'm afraid that in times past I have not been thankful for my many blessings.

8

Trust . . . Three Meals a Day

Our car was sent to Africa *before* the delay Marla caused. A South African man bought it and promised he would pay us the balance owed, about $2,300, upon our arrival. Brother Stairs, our missionary secretary, said, "Pay three months' house rent in advance, buy some secondhand furniture, rent halls for services, and live frugally. Make that money go as far as possible. We will not send any mission funds for three months. We will replace your car later."

We often felt we could have done well if the man's promise materialized, but God had other plans for us. According to his word, we never did arrive, and the money was never paid. What *did* happen was wonderful! Penniless, in a strange land, with five small children, we learned to trust the Lord.

All of us slept in one small bedroom—wall to wall beds. At first, the family with whom we were living served us meals. But because they were struggling financially, too, the lady later said we would have to be responsible for our own meals. I could, however, cook on her coal stove when the servant prepared their food.

About this time I wondered if the Lord still had our address. I then tried *asking* in a simple way. He answered!

"Lord, please send me something to cook for my children." I answered a knock at the door, and there stood Aunt Lil and Uncle Hans Botes.

"We were passing by and thought we would look in . . ." She had a covered basket that she handed to me as she left.

"Some fresh vegetables to cook with your meat."

Well, there wasn't any meat, but that basket came full of vegetables every day for a month, and one cannot starve to death on soup! Years later I learned that "a voice" told her to bring them. She was afraid I would be offended, but my appreciation was obvious.

We spent most of the next two months taking care of other people's homes while they went on holiday. Then a widowed schoolteacher said if we would move to Kempton Park, she would pay the rent and board for us. She also loaned us a deposit on some secondhand furniture. She was soon transferred, so we moved, of necessity, to a cheaper house when our first check came. The next one came seven weeks later, but in the meantime . . .

"Mother, I know it's not quite noon, but the oatmeal we had for breakfast is gone, and we're hungry." Bug looked at the kids for support, and they all nodded.

"What's for lunch?"

"Have you ever heard of Mother Hubbard's cupboard? Go take a look—our shelves are bare! I even used the last grain of salt in the oats."

"Well," Bug said, "I'll walk down to the post office and see if maybe someone sent us a letter with a dollar in it."

I was waiting for his return at the front gate and knew by

the slump of his shoulders that there was no letter—with or without dollars. Watching his approach, I hit bottom. I didn't mind for myself, but my children . . .

"Now, dear," he put a finger under my chin, "don't look like that. God has never failed us. We haven't missed any meals yet. Some of them may have been rather far apart, but we haven't missed any." He came in, and I latched the gate behind him. Just at that instant an African stopped at the gate with the most overloaded basket I'd ever seen on the front of his bicycle. He was pushing the cycle because it was too heavy to ride. I waved him on.

"We didn't order any groceries." He didn't move.

"Is this number 67 Maxwell Street?"

"Yes, but I told you we didn't order groceries."

I leaned over and locked the gate. The Bantu ignored me and looked at Bug.

"Is your name Freeman?" He fumbled in his pocket and came out with the flap of an envelope. He looked at it closely. "Rev. E. L. Freeman, 67 Maxwell Street," he said triumphantly. He handed Bug the scrap of paper. It was our name and address, written with fine spidery flourishes unlike any writing we had ever seen.

"Who sent you?" I asked. He only shrugged his shoulders.

Bug touched my arm. "Dear, I think God has sent our lunch. Will you open the gate and let it come in?"

This was pre-supermarket days in South Africa. Whoever was responsible for that basket had gathered its contents from the butcher, the dairy, the greengrocers and the grocery store. The last of the food was prepared the day our next check came.

Immediately after lunch, I hurried to the only folks we

knew—to say thanks. I was sure they were responsible, but the lady answered, "What a strange and wonderful thing! We didn't know you were in need. We didn't send it."

After that, I asked everyone we had met since our arrival in the country, but no one knew anything about that basket. One day I said to Bug, "I wish I could find the one who sent those groceries; I'd like to thank him adequately or try to, at least. Do you realize our children would have gone hungry otherwise?"

Bug smiled. "Shall I tell you what I think? Do you remember that peculiar handwriting? I think the Lord let us know for sure that He knows exactly where we live. Don't you believe that He still has angels that He dispatches to do his bidding? The One who sent the basket hears us now, so let's go on our knees and thank Him again."

One Sunday night Bug was away in African services. Sandra's throat was painfully sore, but she offered to keep Marla, who had the measles, so I could go to church. I slipped in on the back seat of a little trinity Pentecostal church near us and enjoyed the service even though most of it was in Afrikaans. I was surprised how much I understood. As two were baptized, I leaned forward, listening intently, and was able to understand that the pastor, Piet De Wet, repeated the titles in the ceremony instead of using the NAME they represent. I found myself praying with a loud voice, "O Lord, teach this man the right way to baptize!"

I was the object of many astonished glares, for all of them understood English. I was embarrassed, but my prayer was answered. The next time Pastor De Wet baptized he did it right—in the name of Jesus. He did have a desert experience but came out of it with the truth. Soon after we became friends, he ran from the Lord.

When we heard that he was leaving for Rhodesia without a real reason, I was impressed to say, "Brother De Wet, if God has shown you light and you refuse to walk in it, you will walk in darkness, my brother."

He was reminded of those words by the Spirit until he came back to walk in the light! Later, they founded the church in Benoni. He was faithful for many years until the Lord took him and his lovely wife home, both within a few days.

9

Bug, the Unbeliever

Some of our first African services were held under trees, where the big jets land today. Because of communication difficulties we did not make a lot of progress and were shocked to learn that most of the group we were trying to win actually believed in one of the Black Christs (so-called). They invited Bug to go with them to a meeting at a cinema in Johannesburg to honor their "god." He viewed the proceedings with skepticism, his being the only white face in the midst of many black ones. They sang impressive salutes to their very ordinary looking deity, kissed his feet, and sold "blest" strips of cloth to prevent illness and bottles of salt water to cure all diseases.

The man so honored left his place of prominence and came to Bug, who was sitting on the front row of seats.

"You don't believe in me, do you?"

"No," answered Bug.

"I can prove to you I have great power."

"How?"

"I can reveal all the sins you committed *before* you were converted," assented the man.

"I don't believe it," Bug said. "But what would I have to

do for you to try?"

"Kneel and pray. I will kneel beside you, then I can tell you everything you ever did."

They knelt. Bug praised the Lord for salvation and for the power of Jesus' name. Edward snorted, whistled, and went through several weird gyrations. He then tapped Bug on the shoulder, "You're not cooperating."

"What must I do?"

"Pray harder!"

Bug shifted gears and prayed *louder.* Edward repeated the ritual more vigorously, then he bumped Bug again.

"Cooperate!" he commanded. Bug didn't know anything else to do but praise the Lord as loud as he could. Edward stood up, shaking his head.

"I can't do it."

"I knew you couldn't," Bug said.

"But why? I've revealed the sins of all kinds of people— different stations in life. You are like a closed book. Can you explain this?"

"Yes," Bug answered, "I am probably the first person you have met who has been baptized in the name of Jesus for the remission of sins, according to Acts 2:38. My sins are remitted. God has promised not only to forgive but to forget as well. My sins are gone—never to be remembered. So neither you nor the devil can find them!"

Bug rejoiced all the way home with expanded appreciation for the benefits of full salvation.

W. R. Pair, old friend, missionary, and General Board member, came to visit South Africa not long after we arrived. He hired a car and driver and took Bug for his first visit to Kruger Park. He was entranced by the animals roaming free in their natural habitat and intrigued by "eating all the way through the menu" (food served in courses). The driver was an amiable, middle-aged man, unfortunately illiterate. Bug wondered how he would handle the menu. At the end of each course, when the waiter produced the card for his next choice, he looked as if he studied the list, then with an airy wave of the hand, said, "Bring it!" Whatever came, he ate as though it was what he wanted.

As they were leaving, a group of small black boys, dressed in the barest bit of string and beads, were dancing for them with unbelievable energy and grace. By the time Brother Pair got his movie camera out, they had given up on pennies and quit.

"Tell them to dance again," he said.

The driver obliged in a language they could understand but didn't realize his pistol, which had just been unsealed by park authorities, was still in his hand. He waved his hand (and the pistol), promising them money to dance again. One wave and the boys disappeared so fast it looked as though they melted into the bushes. No amount of calling and promises would bring them back.

10
Content on the Hill

A few weeks later, Bug came in the door laughing. "What in the world is so funny?" I asked.

He could hardly talk, but he waved a yellow piece of paper. "Telegram. Our new car is in Pretoria, and I don't even have two shillings and sixpence to ride the train twenty-five miles to go get it, much less money for petrol (gas). Oh, and it will have to be assembled, too—they shipped it in a box." I laughed with him and wondered if anyone else ever found themselves in such ridiculous circumstances.

Two days later, a lonely dollar came and paid Bug's way to Pretoria. The Lord met all the other needs there, and Bug came home with the wheels that would help us do more for Jesus.

We moved from Kempton Park to a farmhouse on a rocky hill. There were advantages. Being fifteen miles from Pretoria was one—all the government offices we had to deal with were there. It was also a more central location. The children could ride to and from school with a neighbor, and the house was rent free.

There were disadvantages. "Farmhouse" was a misnomer. There wasn't even a tiny garden spot. I was sure there must be some soil under all those rocks, but if there was, I failed to find it. We did not have electricity or running water—unless the one who brought it from the spring at the foot of the hill felt like running! We learned speedily to get our water supply early. There were several African families living near, and they followed the age-old custom of using any water supply as a bathtub and washtub.

One afternoon Dale chose to play with some little black friends while we went grocery shopping. On our return he proudly informed us that he and "another pickaninny" had killed a big snake. They were trying to catch "widow birds"—small, black birds whose tail plumage becomes so lush in the autumn that they fly low, skimming barely above the tasseled heads of grass. Dale lunged for what he thought was a bird. His friend saw the ominous, flicking snake's tongue and pulled him over backwards to safety. They retreated to a safe distance and killed the snake by throwing stones. The black boy said it was a bad kind, so they burned it. But there was enough of the remains for a neighbor to identify it as a spitting cobra. Their venom, usually aimed with deadly accuracy for the eyes, causes blindness. We shuddered as we thanked God for His protection.

Dining by candlelight may be romantic, but *living* by candlelight is frustrating, unhandy, and messy. Everything we owned gradually acquired spots from blobs of melted candle wax. The captain of our boat had told us in parting, "I hope we meet again someday, and then maybe you can tell me what this country does with the tons and tons of paraffin wax that our ships unload here."

It didn't take long to learn that candles and floor polish

were the answer to his question. Many things were not available just after the war, and kerosene lamps were on that list.

I wish it were possible to record all the miracles of answered prayer. Sharon had a dangerous fall on the cement floor one night, hitting her head extremely hard. Blood foamed from her ears and poured from her nose. We took her and the concussion symptoms to our ever attentive Friend. The next day she was her usual, happy, three-year-old self!

Bug originated a little joke about my being unhappy in heaven if I had no washing to do, but getting laundry done on the farm was anything but a joke. I tried taking the bundle down to the spring to wash, but the water was so hard it needed treating before the clothes would come clean. I found a big, black, three-legged pot—the Africans used them for cooking enormous quantities of their staple "pap" (cornmeal porridge).

I remembered my mother's boiling water and adding a couple of tablespoons of lye to "break" the hard water in West Texas. My first hassle was learning to ask for "caustic soda," not lye, but it worked. Rinsing required taking the washed clothes down the hill to the spring or carrying the water up. The total effort was so exhausting I was eventually compelled to hire one of the many native women who came daily looking for work.

I thought at first I had made a good choice. She was hardworking and efficient though communication consisted of gestures and demonstrations. Then I noticed it was increasingly difficult to match socks, and panties for the girls were suddenly in short supply. I came around the corner one day as she threw a handful of socks on the fire under the pot. I paid her for the work she had done and took over the washing again. All I could understand of her reasons was "too much!"

I was in tears and complained to Bug.

"Why don't you ask the Lord for a washing machine? The Bible plainly says 'ye have not, because ye ask not.'"

I made a catty remark that I'd have to ask for a power station, too, and stormed out. Later, I realized my frustrated bitterness only made my situation more intolerable. Just one good prayer meeting changed all that, and in amazing mercy, Jesus let me know He still had my address, even on that desolate, rocky hill.

Someone had given me a case of toilet soap to bring to Africa with us. It was a blessing when our freight finally caught up with us. But laundry soap was rationed, and I could never get enough. The owner of a cafe gave me a four-gallon can of very black oil that had been used for frying potatoes and fish until it was too rancid and burnt. I boiled it with water, strained it several times, and tried my mother's homemade soap recipe. It worked beautifully, and the laundry soap problem was solved.

When the winter mornings were garnished with thick, white frost, I felt so sorry for a little black boy, attired with but a string around his waist, who shivered past my front door herding cattle every day. I found some used clothing that would fit him, and joy was unbounded. But the next morning the string was all he had on! I sent for his mother to explain to me why he wasn't wearing the clothes. Her explanation was very simple. His sister would be married shortly, and he needed the clothes for the wedding. There was no need to wear them out by *wearing* them!

Bug was asked to come and "bless" the bride and

groom in the third ceremony they went through to be married. Prayer was requested because this was the "religious" ceremony. The *traditional* and *civil* ceremonies were already completed. The wagon bringing the bride stopped near our house, and I had no success keeping my clan otherwise occupied. They were fascinated by the customs and ways of the Africans. Actually, the pair is considered married from the first ceremony. Financial reasons often postpone the last two rituals, spreading the whole affair over several months or even years.

The bride was disrobed, and water was poured over her. Then, layer by layer, she dressed in petticoats of different colors, topped off by a full-skirted dress of white net. For some reason, this whole performance was repeated three times. Then, according to previous arrangements, Bug was called to give his "blessing." The bride walked the equivalent of two blocks while the older women encircled her, undulating in an attempt to sweep with large branches the evil spirits and troubles from the air and ground.

Only a prayer was required from Bug, which was just as well, for they didn't understand a word he said anyway. It was evident that they wanted us to leave as soon as the prayer was ended. Their attitude spoke plainly enough: "Thanks for the prayer, and good-bye." We left. Later, when the festivities grew progressively louder and wilder around the beer pots, we understood why.

Careful planning was required to combat the dreary prospects of our first Christmas in Africa. It was surprising to learn that this joyous occasion could be completely divorced from finance. We cheerfully started the children on small gift-making projects. Whispered consultations and guarded doors added to a genial air of conspiracy and excitement.

Content on the Hill

Bug found a leafless thorn tree in the veldt whose multiple bone white, three-inch-long thorns gave it a sort of stark (and sticky!) attractiveness. Someone sent a package of multicolored gum drops and some "angel hair," so Bug and I impaled a gum drop on each thorn and wrapped the whole tree in angel hair. The children were entranced by the shimmering transformation and declared it was the loveliest Christmas tree ever!

We sang carols on Christmas Eve, by candlelight. The nearest resemblance to a Christmas spirit came when Bug read the beautiful, old story of the Nativity. We sang again and prayed together on Christmas morning. Opening the interesting packages ended suspense and revealed considerable ingenuity and resourcefulness. Since December is in the middle of summer in South Africa, salads were more appropriate than the usual rich, traditional dishes. Our dinner was not elaborate but sufficient, and we were thankful when the holiday hurdle passed without one child's expressing homesickness.

For several days a scriptural phrase reoccurred in my thoughts: ". . . whatsoever state . . . whatsoever state. . . ." When I finally took time to read the rest of the verse, it was, "for I have learned, in whatsoever state I am, therewith to be content" (Philippians 4:11). Ouch!

It was easy to decide that my family needed a mother and wife with a contented heart. It was, however, harder to accomplish. I tried to lecture myself into contentment. It didn't work. But when I backed up far enough to confess and ask forgiveness for my shortcoming, it happened. I was amazed to see the peaceful submission of my new attitude reflected in better behavior by my offspring, and I was willing to spend the rest of my life on that rocky hill.

11

Old Jack and His Wives

We won the confidence of our African neighbors by small acts of love and kindness, so they invited us to witness a *manhood ritual* that is seldom seen by outsiders. Fierce-looking young men, smeared with white clay and dressed in loincloths, joined in combat. They were armed with long, flexible, but tough wattle sticks and small cowhide shields. They were not playing games but attacked each other with the vicious intent of slicing backs and shoulders to ribbons. There were referees that prevented a man being hit when he was down. Seemingly, I was the only one perturbed by the blood that splattered every direction with telling blows. "If blood qualified for manhood, a large number of them made the grade," I thought as I washed it out of my hair later, feeling slightly nauseated.

Bug was becoming increasingly concerned about our schoolchildren. They left before daylight each morning and didn't return until our neighbor's business endeavors were completed and he brought his children and ours home. It was usually after dark. At first I didn't realize that the nice house in Pretoria, with low rent, that suddenly became available was a direct answer to prayer. When I received a letter from Jewell Stanton, then pastor in Orange, Texas, that the church was sending money for a washing machine, Bug was not surprised. He had prayed for that, too.

We continued making regular trips to anyplace the doors were open to hold services. Our first converts were from a group that met regularly on a farm about twenty-five miles from town. Old Jack had two wives. To our amazement, all three were filled with the Holy Ghost in one service. They needed to be baptized in water, but Bug was perplexed. After all, a man with two wives! Old Jack solved the problem.

"Moruti, it would be against our custom for my second wife to be sent away. She is the mother of my children, and besides, she has no living family. She must stay in my kraal, and we will take care of her. She will become my sister, and I will live only with my first wife. When you baptize us, I will enter the water first alone, and after I am baptized, then you can baptize the women." So it was.

* * * *

"You are twelve years old; it's time you went to the initiation school." The strident voice of Esther grated on the ears of her son, Ernest Shai. He could not explain his reasons, but his whole being revolted against following the age-old custom of his tribe: joining the other boys of the village with the witch doctor, in an isolated place to learn the ancient traditions, taboos, and witch lore of his Sepedi nation. He knew only a soft answer would divert his mother's determination, so he pled gently.

"Please, Mother, I don't want to leave you. Let me wait until next year—I'll go then." She agreed but made it very clear that there would not be another postponement. When his thirteenth birthday was near, Ernest realized there was only one thing to be done. He rolled his blanket into a tight roll, took some leftover porridge, a small gourd for dipping water, and a little dried meat. When the first gray light of early dawn crept over the mountains that ringed Sabie, he left his mother's kraal. He thought of Johannesburg and the mines, nearly three hundred miles away.

"I am strong. I can work, and I will not go for the initiation."

It took considerable courage for a boy who had never been more than five miles from home to brave wild animals, strange tribes, frosty nights on the high veldt, and the unknown perils of a large city.

If some of his tribesmen had not befriended him, he might not have made it. He survived by odd jobs and his wits until he had enough experience and age to hold down a good job. Then he met Marie, a vivacious girl from the Cape. They were married. They both worked, and life was satisfying for Ernest and Marie. One day he passed by an odd, little group holding services on a street corner. He paused to listen, and the Word of God went like an arrow straight to his heart, and tears streamed down his face. Before he realized what was happening, he was on his knees getting personally acquainted with Jesus.

Marie's heart was hungry, and she was glad to learn more about the Lord. They went to church, and a new joy and fulfillment graced their lives as they eagerly studied the Bible together. But gradually, both of them felt a nagging uneasiness that neither understood at first. Ernest pushed back his plate, "Sorry, Marie, I'm just not hungry." Then she would hear him praying and weeping. They tried in vain to satisfy the increasing burden by stepped-up activity in the church. But a day came when Ernest could no longer stall.

"Marie, the Lord is calling me to take the gospel to Sabie. It will mean sacrifice and maybe even danger, but . . ."

"It's all right, Ernest; Jesus has spoken to me, too. I *know* we must go, and I'm willing. It would be better if I had the Holy Ghost, but I'll keep seeking."

Just before they left for Sabie, someone handed Ernest a tract on baptism in the name of Jesus. He immediately understood the scriptures. Not long after their arrival in Sabie, God sent a man to baptize Ernest Shai according to Acts 2:38.

The early part of Shai's story was supplied by Marie, but from the beginning of his work in Sabie, we were there for regular, gratifying visits.

Shai (as we always called him) discovered what he was up against his second day in Sabie. His mother invited them for a visit and graciously pulled out a beautiful leopard skin for Marie to sit on. Immediately, her head pulled backwards, her arms and legs twisted into terrifying cramps. She gasped, "Shai, help me! Help me!" He pulled her from the skin, calling on the name of Jesus.

He sternly asked his mother, "What does this mean?" Esther evaded his question and pretended to be concerned about Marie. That visit terminated quickly.

"I suspect my mother has become a witch doctor since I left home. That skin is probably consecrated to the devil, Marie. It could not have affected you if you were filled with the Holy Ghost. We must fast and pray until you receive the protection of the Spirit," said Shai.

The following day, Esther sent Marie some sugar, a scarcity and a welcome gift. But when she wanted to put some in her tea, the Lord whispered to her, "Don't use it—poison." She threw it away.

Shai held services in different huts. Marie received her baptism in the Spirit, and this was the start of revival. Late one bright, moonlit night, Shai heard his name being called softly, over and over. He went to investigate. It was Esther.

"Son, I want to talk to you."

"Yes, Mother."

"This Jesus you preach about—does He forgive all sinners?"

"He does, Mother."

"Will he forgive terrible sins—like murder?"

Shai felt a tenderness for his mother and took her hand. "Though your sins be as scarlet, they shall be white as snow! If the sinner is willing to repent, Jesus is merciful, and He will forgive all sins, no matter how terrible."

Esther wept for a long time.

"Sit here on this log, Son. I have a long story to tell you—a sad, true story." She stared in the direction of some dark shadows for a long time, then began to speak softly—so softly he strained to hear.

"I wanted to be a witch doctor long before you left. When you were gone, I went to the head witch doctor and asked that he teach me. Your father objected, so I poisoned him. . . ." Her voice trailed away. They sat in silence. Finally she spoke again.

"I took another man who was agreeable that I learn witchcraft. I was a good student and did everything my instructor asked. I was expecting a child when I was told that the demons wanted the heart of a newborn baby. I made my plans ahead of time, and as soon as my baby was born, I cut out its heart with a sharp knife." She shuddered and went on.

"There were many strange rituals required of me. My second baby was allowed to live longer, but when it was six weeks old, my teacher informed me the demons demanded the liver of a baby that age. There were three other children, and I sacrificed all of them to Satan to obtain power." She sat with bowed head.

"Many other wicked things I have done, and none of them bothered me until you came back. Now, my evil deeds torment me. I feel the warm blood of my babies on my hands, and regret cuts my heart like a knife. Will Jesus forgive me? Is there mercy for such a wicked woman as I have been?" She sobbed.

Shai gently introduced Esther to God's infinite mercy, explained genuine repentance and the plan of salvation. They knelt together by the log while Esther asked the Lord for mercy and Shai asked for her deliverance in the name of Jesus.

"Son, there's a lot of things I need to get rid of. How should it be done?"

"There's only one way—they must be burned. Bring them out, and I'll get the matches and kerosene."

Esther went into the devil house, piled her fetishes, sacrifices, and artifacts of witchcraft on the leopard skin, and pulled it out to where Shai waited. He poured on the kerosene and struck a match. Green, foul smelling flames leaped high while Esther and Shai walked around the fire, praising God. When the fire burned to ashes, he took her to the river and baptized her in the name of Jesus. They decided the devil house should be cleaned and consecrated for a church. Before the new congregation outgrew the small building (and converted it to a parsonage), Esther was filled with the Holy Spirit and worshiped God in the very place she had formerly offered sacrifices to spirits.

The office of witch doctor is lucrative, but Esther happily changed her occupation to that of a basket maker—tedious work with small remuneration. She has been a testimony to the grace of God ever since.

12

Africa, the Beautiful

Our children thoroughly enjoyed frequent trips to Sabie. We always managed a picnic and some sightseeing between services. Sabie and Pilgrims Rest are about twenty-two miles apart, situated beautifully in mountains rich with historical and scenic attractions. We visited Fairyland, Mac Mac Falls, gold and asbestos mines, and a variety of grotesque, awe-inspiring rock formations. There was a place on the main road between the two towns where a powerful magnetic force held the car, barely allowing it to coast down the sharp incline. On the return journey we were pulled rapidly up the hill even though Bud had removed his foot from the accelerator.

One day we watched people staking out gold mining claims in a large valley. Everyone waited on the highway until a gun was fired, giving the signal for those participating to scramble, run, and stumble down the hill with stakes in their hands.

Our favorite spot was Lone Creek Falls, three miles from Sabie. It looked like what many people picture all of Africa looking like—nestled in a deep ravine, with crystal clear water plummeting from incredible heights against an intriguing background of lichen-covered rocks, tall trees, dense shrubbery, and tangled vines. Picnics were special in that glossy green setting.

The church in Sabie needed a building. Shai made a large quantity of sun-dried mud blocks. The children helped with rummage sales to buy the roofing and steel windows. Peter and Marie Jensen, independent missionaries, offered to go help with the building. A competent lady, who was staying with us temporarily, offered to take care of the children. We loaded a small trailer with building materials and a tent since we did not want to impose on genial hosts who had offered short term hospitality to our family in the past. This was going to take longer!

Work progressed well. The men thought everything would be completed in a week or less. We enjoyed camping in a lovely site on the bank of the Sabie River. Friday afternoon an uneasy feeling began that haunted me the rest of the weekend in spite of wonderful services. We reserved telephoning strictly for emergencies, but I ached to call home. Marie teased me about being lonesome for the kids. I hoped that was all. Later Sunday night, bright lights shone on our tent. It was the police. They brought an urgent message to phone home at once.

When I finally got through, my friend said, "It's Sharon. She developed a sudden high fever and in the night, Friday, started screaming for the lights to be turned on. They were on, Nona. Her right arm and leg are unnaturally white and paralyzed. Like you, I'm a stranger to Pretoria and didn't know a doctor to call. I've just prayed; that was all I knew to do. I thought the police would never find you. I do hope you can start home right away."

"We'll be on our way home as soon as we can load up. Does she still seem to be blind?"

"She keeps begging for the lights to be turned on. She is so hot with fever. Oh, hurry, and PRAY!"

In short order, we were loaded and zigzagged up three miles of hairpin curves, out of Sabie valley. We had 225 miles and four more mountain passes to make. The Chevrolet fairly flew, and the little trailer danced along behind us. Eighty miles from home, at Middleburg, Bug stopped for a break. I had prayed nonstop for Sharon and our safety, but just as he opened the car door, I *knew!*

"You can slow down, dear; Sharon is okay!"

"Praise the Lord!" he answered. "You've heard from Him, too. Jesus whispered peace to my heart as I walked back to the car."

We drove in our yard just before dawn. A weary but happy friend met us.

"She has been sleeping normally for over an hour, and the fever is gone!"

I tiptoed to her bed, and the blue eyes flew open. "Oh, Mommy, you've come home!" She reached up for me with *both* arms. Two of my questions were answered in that moment. We did not have the benefit of a doctor's diagnosis though we knew there was still an epidemic of polio in the Pretoria area. She was weak for a few days but soon back to the usual activities of a four-year-old girl.

Missionaries of a Canadian organization came by with their six-year-old grandson. The lady was congenial, the man controversial, but we carefully avoided clashes and enjoyed his ministry and the fellowship. They were on their way to Southern Rhodesia. Our house seemed very quiet when they left after a two months' stay.

Six weeks later, they returned. She came to me in the kitchen early one morning.

"Sister Freeman, I know you are wondering why we did not stay in Rhodesia. I simply couldn't stand it. I dreamed my husband died. I didn't tell him, but I kept insisting that we come back so we could be with you folks in case anything happened. I dreamed the same thing again last night."

Tears streamed down her face. I tried to comfort her. "Perhaps your dreams are the results of anxiety. You should know you are welcome here. Please don't be afraid. Maybe the enemy is trying to torment you."

A tent was bought and services held. Many plans were made for "after Christmas." I was so involved in baking and planning small gifts for the children that I forgot my friend's ominous dreams. I was thankful to have visitors (I thought to myself). Our second Christmas in Africa would not be lonely like that first one on the farm.

The preacher visited a mine on Wednesday of Christmas week and returned late with a sore throat. He spent most of the next two days in bed and seemed more miserable than actually sick.

Saturday was Christmas Eve, and he sent for me. "I'm not really sick, just my throat is painful, but I think you should call a doctor. Maybe it would be best for me to go to the hospital. I'd hate to spoil Christmas for these youngsters."

Doctors are listed alphabetically, but I soon discovered there was a problem finding one willing to make a house call to an unknown patient on the day before Christmas. I started at *A* and went through the list to *V* before I found one who agreed to come. After the examination, the doctor called Bug and me aside.

"He has a throat infection. I don't think it's serious, but under the circumstances, it would probably be wise for him to spend a few days in the hospital."

Two o'clock in the afternoon, arrangements were completed, and he put on his dressing gown and walked to the car. Bug took him to Pretoria General Hospital and stayed with him until he was assigned a room.

"Look, friend," he said, "I'm all right. I just need rest, so there is no need for you to stay."

Bug took the man's wife to see him at visiting hours— 7:00 P.M. He said he wanted to sleep, so they didn't stay long. It was pouring rain. I had promised to play the accordion for a group of young people going caroling, but when the rain increased, they decided to sing at our house. I served refreshments and really enjoyed having them though I could not understand an unaccountable heartache. Tears kept falling—I didn't know why. We phoned the hospital at 10:00 P.M. They said the preacher was sleeping.

Just before the crowd left, after 11:00 P.M., Sandra came to see me. "Mother, I don't feel good. My throat is very sore." I helped her undress for bed. She was hot with fever, so I called Bug, and we prayed for her. I fell wearily in the bed about midnight. At 2:00 A.M. the phone rang.

"Mrs. Freeman, I'm phoning from the hospital. A gentleman from your address was admitted to the hospital yesterday afternoon. . . ." She paused.

"Yes?"

"Is his wife with you?"

"Yes."

"Well, tell her that her husband has died."

Somehow, I got back to the bedroom.

"What's wrong?" Bug asked. "Was that someone from

the hospital calling?" Choked with shock, I couldn't get a word out but nodded assent.

"Is he worse?" I nodded.

"Oh no, don't tell me he's dead!" I nodded again. I felt numb. Bug put my housecoat around me.

"Look, honey, pull yourself together. You'll have to go tell her." I couldn't move, so he led me down the hall to her room and knocked on her door. When she answered, I went in. She was sitting up in bed, and I put my arms around her.

She said, "That was the hospital phoning, wasn't it? I know my husband has gone. . . ."

Finally, my vocal chords worked, "I'm so very sorry." We wept together. Her greatest comfort was that the Lord had warned her it would happen.

Death was caused by diphtheria and heart failure. By daylight a provincial nurse had arrived to inoculate all the children. Sandra had every symptom of diphtheria, and three of the other children had sore throats and were feverish. A pall of gloom enveloped us. The children listlessly opened their gifts in the late afternoon. Preparations for Christmas dinner stopped; no one felt like eating. We gave the cakes and pies to visitors who came to express sympathy or offer help.

By Monday night, Sandra was critically ill, no longer able to swallow even water. We never felt a more urgent need of contact with the Lord. We had prayed several times, but one desperate prayer got through, and she was instantly touched by divine healing power. We prayed for the other children then, and all of them were healed.

The funeral delay caused by the holiday season was tedious. The preacher's wife stayed with us a month afterward, winding up their affairs. We were able to assist her with untangling complications to avoid probation of her husband's will in three different countries.

Our international airport at Palmietfontein was a ramshackle, ex-army barracks affair then. Seven carloads of us were there to give the lady a loving send-off. Departure time was near when the grandson indicated he needed a restroom. We waited. The plane was called. Bug sent me to see why she had not returned. I looked in and reported, "No one in sight."

He said, "Go *call* her, dummy." When I called her name, she answered.

"Oh, Sister Freeman, help me! The door locked when I closed it. My grandson has claustrophobia and is about to faint. Can you get him out and call for help?" The cubicle was enclosed all the way to the floor. I went next door and stood on the closed lid of the commode and managed to pull him over the top of the wall. I turned him over to Bug and found a stewardess who brought a bunch of keys. None of them fit the lock, so she called two burly policemen, who put their shoulders against the door . . . at the count of three: "One, two, three, heave!"

By this time most of the farewell group was in the ladies' restroom. The loudspeaker droned on and on, "Passengers en route to Canada, please clear customs and immigration."

"One, two, three, heave!" But the door did not give.

Aunt Lil tugged at her tall husband's hand. "Come on, Hans, you're the only one to open that door." He came reluctantly, mumbling about his dislike of going in ladies' restrooms. There was quite a crowd in there by then, including several airport officials.

"One, two, three, heave!" He watched as the police tried again without success.

"Out of the way, boys," he said. "Sister, step back away from the door." Few of us could believe what we saw. Uncle Hans put his hands in his pockets, ducked his head, and rammed the door with his bald head. It was done effortlessly, no straining or obvious force, but the door flew open.

Her name was still being called over and over on the loudspeaker. There was no time for good-byes. She grabbed her grandson and took off for the departing passengers' exit so fast the little fellow's feet were flying! We all stood silent though we recovered enough to wave to them as they went up the steps to board the plane. I think our hilarity after- wards was partly the release of tensions and the strain of the past few weeks.

I had recurrent nightmares that persisted for six weeks. I would dream of the phone ringing and hurry to answer — hear again the nurse's brusque death message and awaken suddenly, trembling with violent stomach cramps. I could hardly eat, and nothing I ate stayed with me long. I almost despaired of victory. But one night Bug reminded the enemy that I belonged to Jesus and forbade him to torment God's property any longer. That was my first peaceful night, and the next day I was able to eat and soon regained strength.

13

Welcome, Dr. Buck

We received a letter from Dr. Buck, advising us to expect him shortly. He was the dentist who sold his practice in England and went to Central Africa to make a set of teeth for Missionary C. T. Studd. We had barely read the letter when a phone call announced he was waiting for us at the train station. "And bring your lorry (truck) please; I have thirty-four pieces of luggage!"

The small, wiry man was a ludicrous sight in modern Pretoria, attired in tropical short pants, cork helmet, and swinging a storm lantern in his hand as he marched up and down the platform. We did not have a "lorry," but our trusty tent-hauling trailer conveyed him and his mountain of baggage to our house.

He promptly set up his portable dental equipment in our living room and began working on the teeth of anyone he could inveigle to sit in the crude, portable chair that had traveled with him up and down Africa. There was no time for my teeth to be checked (fortunately). I had three other sets of visitors, and my days were fully occupied with meals and laundry, besides services every night.

He decided that Sam Jensen could cap a tooth for him. Sam was a good carpenter and well acquainted with a larger sort of drill but had never had his hands in someone else's mouth before. The sights and sounds of that operation are unforgettable. My children encouraged quite a few spectators, and when Dr. Buck would give instructions, interspersed with sudden yelps to Sam, who had the drill and both hands in the doctor's mouth, they all dissolved on the floor in helpless laughter. When I realized that the patience of both men was becoming strained, I shooed their audience out.

Dr. Buck decided the Transvaal's weather was too cold and moved to Durban, eventually leaving South Africa for other climates. We regretted his departure, for we learned to love him and appreciated his burden for a lost world.

The C. S. Curries, headed for Rhodesia, were our pleasant guests for nearly three months. Our friendship deepened and was a mutual source of pleasure and enjoyment for many years. His magnificent sermons were a delight—120 were filled with the Holy Ghost in one revival held in Pretoria.

Bug solved the problem of the continual second (or third) table for the children by having a small table made for them so they could eat at the same time the adults did in our large dining room. Each child had a week's turn at saying grace. Sandra was able to ad lib her prayers, but for the rest, I taught a simple table grace:

Lord, we thank You for this food. Bless it to the nourishment of our body. Provide for those who have no food. In Jesus' name, amen.

Welcome, Dr. Buck

During one of Dale's weeks, I noticed that his prayer was shortened by a few words at each meal. I waited to see how far he would go. When, on Friday night, he bowed his head and said, "Bless it, amen," I decided it was time to intervene and restore him to "proper grace!"

In response to the Curries' call for help in Southern Rhodesia, Bug and Jeremiah (an African preacher and interpreter) took the big, three pole tent on a trailer to Salisbury. The total trip was 780 miles (about 90 miles tarred, over 400 miles of narrow cement strips, and the rest washboard gravel). There was some similarity to towing a bucking horse as the trailer bounced and jigged over bumpy surfaces. They arrived with only one mishap—the tent was soaked from rainstorms. This was a blessing in disguise, however, for when permission to erect the tent was refused, they pleaded, "It must go up to dry out." Once up, it stayed up!

When Bug and Jeremiah had to leave, the tent was quietly and quickly exchanged for one bought by Brother Currie. Meetings went on without interruption. Three years later, it was "dry" enough to be taken down—when a building was ready to house the church.

What meetings they had while they were in Rhodesia! Each evening, shortly before service, Bug would pull the trailer through the crowded, narrow streets of Salisbury. Esther Currie, truly a remarkable woman, would sit perched on a stool, playing her accordion. Droves of people were led to the tent in this Pied Piper fashion.

When Bug was certain the Curries were well on their way to opening a new work, he and Jeremiah started for home. He was still hoping to cross the border before the 8:00 P.M. deadline when a trailer wheel rolled off into the bushes—ten miles short of their goal.

"Well, Jeremiah," he said, "we've no choice but to sleep in the car. Take the back seat, my friend—you'll have more room there. I'll bunk up here in the front."

Many years later Bug was told: "Do you know when we learned that you truly loved the Africans? It was when you shared the car with Jeremiah and did not push him out with the lions."

14

Bout with Leukemia

We were not unhappy in the big house, but seeping springs under the foundation caused excessive moisture and mustiness, and it seemed that at all times one or more of the children had a terribly unhealthy cold. Lynda had pneumonia four times, herself.

So we were thankful to relocate in Capital Park, in a north-facing house built against a hill. The children loved exploring the hill, as well as nearby Apies River, a rather insignificant, little stream that only qualified for the title "river" in times of torrential rainfall. This was 1950 and our eighth move since arriving in South Africa.

The entire family had improved health in our new location—except me. Gradually, there were more and more things I was too weak to attempt. A failing appetite resulted in lost weight, and my skin developed a yellowish transparency. I could make evening service only if I rested all day. Bug wrote the Missions Department for advice; they suggested medical attention immediately.

On the first examination, Dr. R. Du Plessis said I had pernicious anemia and recommended I try an especially nutritious diet for a month. During that time, my glands became noticeably enlarged. The muscular cramps that plagued me for months became more frequent and painful.

After the second examination, his diagnosis was leukemia.

"Mrs. Freeman, you asked me to be frank and truthful. I really think you should return to the States; they could probably keep you alive longer."

"No, I won't consider returning. How long do you think I will live, Doctor?"

"If treatment is begun right away, I believe I can promise you a year."

"And if I don't take the treatment, how long?"

He shrugged his shoulders—"Maybe six months."

"What *is* the treatment you suggest? I am extremely allergic to drugs."

"There are no drugs involved at the beginning. We should start with daily liver injections and weekly blood transfusions, spaced as necessary."

"But, Doctor, we are missionaries, and there are no funds available for treatment. But if I take the treatment, what will I be able to do?"

"Do?" He leaned forward over his desk. "Dear lady, don't you understand? Your days of doing are over. No doubt you have been faithful, but someone else will have to take your place now. It is important for you to realize you have preached your last sermon and driven your last mile in gospel work."

I sat still in unbelieving silence. The doctor continued: "I don't know how you managed to get to my office. I have seen people with blood pressure as low as yours but none of them walking around. Look, I'll give you the medication;

you get a hypodermic needle and give yourself the treatment."

He handed Bug a bottle containing ten cc's of liver concentrate. "Bring her to the hospital on Wednesday for the first transfusion."

At home, Bug asked, "Shouldn't I write the churches at home for prayer?"

"No! We finally get to the field in '48, and by early '51 I'm dying? It's disgusting! I'm so ashamed; please don't write anyone."

Bug didn't answer, but he remembered a good preacher friend who once said, "If ever you need prayer for a special need, let me know. I may not write, but I will pray." A letter with details of my condition was mailed to Ralph Glasgow the next day without my knowledge.

I made a decision. "Honey, return this hypo needle to the drugstore. Exchange it for soap or something we need. I'm not going to start the injections or transfusions. I want to put myself in God's hands, and whatever He does is good."

The next two weeks were blurry with pain. I couldn't pray for myself but felt at peace when I was able to think at all.

Then, one day was so rough, I prayed, "Oh dear Jesus, don't let me see the light of another day. Please, Lord, if it is Your will, take me home."

But in the night I had a strange but vivid dream. I was in the States in a home with wooden walls (South African homes are masonry because of a timber shortage). I saw a man kneeling. I thought, "It will be so wonderful to hear someone pray." I tiptoed nearer and recognized Ralph Glasgow's voice! As he rebuked the disease that was ravaging my body, in the name of Jesus, I felt an electric-like shock go through me from head to toe. I was immediately awake with clarity of mind, all pain and discomfort gone. I seemed to float lightly in a new consciousness of God's love.

I tried to arouse Bug to share the wonderful news with him, but he was weary and slept soundly. Then love closed my eyes in deep restful sleep. I waked to bright sunlight. Listening to the house sounds, I realized I had slept through the schoolchildren getting off. The two little girls were playing happily outside, and I could hear Bug in the kitchen. I had not dressed myself without help for six months, but I was healed! Somehow, I knew the weakness would gradually be replaced by strength.

When I got to the kitchen, fully dressed but holding on to things for support, Bug said, "Honey, I wanted you to rest. . . ." Then he noticed. "You are dressed!"

"Yes, dear, let me tell you the good news—I'm healed!" I told him about my dream, and we marveled together when we compared the dream with the letter he wrote.

"Well, you are still pale, but we believe God. Let's kneel right here and thank Him for the miracle."

That night I went to church and testified of my healing. Every day after that I grew stronger. Since that day I've been amazed each time I consider the unfathomable mercy of my lovely Jesus. I now know how Hezekiah the king must have felt when the sentence of death was given him by the prophet, followed by God's graciously adding years to his life when he prayed.

15

Rosie's Wait

God gave me a special love and burden for the Colored people (mulattoes) who lived to themselves because they were rejected by both the blacks and whites.

Bug was away so much, opening up the African work in every possible direction, that I couldn't depend on having the car. But I found I could ride the bus to Claremont, a Colored slumlike area nearby. I went from door to door several Sunday afternoons, trying to find an opening. Many adults were too drunk to understand what I was saying, but I knew the gospel could lift these precious souls if I could only bring it to them.

I turned in at one gate, and the Spirit whispered, "This is your open door." I noticed what an ideal place the large porch would be. Enclosed on three sides, there would be protection from burning sun or icy wind. Confidently, I brought my plea for the children to the neat lady who answered my knock. I couldn't believe my ears when she answered with a flat "No!" Surely she didn't understand. I reworded my request.

"I want to start a Sunday school for all these children

who are growing up without God. I could hold it under the tree in your yard . . . or . . . on your porch. . . ."

"No!" she answered firmly the second time. I remembered the Spirit's whisper, so I stalled for time and asked for a drink of water. When Rosie Jacobs brought the glass of water, I asked her to please reconsider. She still said "No," but there was a puzzled look on her face.

"What do you teach? How does your church baptize?" It was a relief to answer. The words tumbled out.

"We teach the Bible. We teach about Jesus. We baptize according to Peter's message on the Day of Pentecost. 'Repent, and be baptized every one of you in the name of Jesus Christ for the remission of sins!'"

That was as far as I got. She fell to her knees before me and kissed my hands while tears streamed down her face.

"At last," she wept, "you have come! We've waited so long. I had lost hope."

I lifted her up, and she told me the incredible story of her father. He had been a denominational preacher but had become discouraged and had given up. God had dealt with him through sickness, and in his urgent search to really know the Lord, great Bible truths had been revealed to him. He had taught his family that Jesus is the only true God and Savior and had baptized them in the name of Jesus as the disciples proclaimed on the birthday of the church. When he was dying, he had exacted a solemn promise from his family— that they would never allow anyone to hold services in their home who did not understand Jesus Name baptism.

He prophesied, "People will come from across the sea. They will strengthen you in the truth and baptize your children in the name of Jesus."

She had waited twelve years.

The Sunday school started the next Sunday and was alternately both my joy and despair. The attendance swung unpredictably from 15 to 150. I soon learned that an impromptu ball game or a wedding or a funeral or an interesting family fight could make my pupils forget their classes. But I plugged away. Every Sunday afternoon at 3:00 I was there. A scripture often came to mind: "my word . . . shall not return unto me void, but it shall accomplish that which I please, and . . . prosper . . ." (Isaiah 55:11).

There had to be some good ground where the seed of the Word would take root. Interest grew, and regular Friday night Bible studies started. When Bug saw the people were really hungry for more of the Lord, the tent went up for the first of many evangelistic efforts in that area. It was almost like the birth of an instant church as fifty-one were filled with the Holy Spirit.

We look back now on a memory—brocade of rich blessings, a little pathos, and a few chuckles. Sandra and I sat side by side one night, playing our accordions, when she looked back and I saw her eyes widen. "Mother," she whispered, "there's a gun barrel stuck through a hole in the tent—p-p-pointing right at our backs."

I glanced back and probably turned pale but whispered, "We can't afford to panic, honey. These folks are so excitable—keep playing!"

I caught Bug's eye and indicated our problem. He moved casually to the front of the tent (we found it best to have only one exit) and ran to the area of the hole. But the culprit scrambled into the darkness and found cover in a shallow ditch.

While we sang the same chorus over and over in the tent, a determined sleuth covered the terrain thoroughly in search of the culprit. When Bug spotted his quarry and closed in, bravado was gone, for the fifteen-year-old boy was reciting the Lord's Prayer with a decided quiver in his voice.

He didn't receive forgiveness immediately. Bug hauled him out by the collar and the seat of his pants and marched him, gun and all, back into the tent. He gave him a seat of honor at his side for the rest of the service. Forgiveness was easier when we realized the gun would only shoot pellets. But it did look authentic!

Then there was the time I was praying with a seeker. I didn't realize I presented a tempting target backed up against the canvas. We never did learn who administered the kick that sent me tumbling and left me with a dilly of a bruise. Education can be painful and costly!

16

The Tent Ministry

When the tent went up in a new area, one small boy was an interested spectator. He watched and listened through one of the numerous holes in the canvas side curtains. Suddenly, he understood what was happening in the tent and ran home.

"Mother! Mother!" he yelled excitedly, "You must come to the tent! Quickly! There's a big man named Jesus with curly hair and glasses. He puts his hands on sick people and makes them well!"

His mother had long ago despaired of ever being well again. She was one of eight persons in the whole country who suffered from a rare, incurable disease; her condition was steadily deteriorating. She was not able to do anything "quickly," but with the help of family and friends she got to the tent and learned that her most urgent need was salvation for her soul. The big man was not Jesus, but when Bug and Hans Botes prayed for Katie in that wonderful name, she was instantly healed. She soon became one of the happy redeemed.

Katie ignored repeated notices from the medical

authorities to come in for a checkup. Finally, the police arrived to escort her to the hospital. They said her file *must* be brought up to date. She was compelled to go though she insisted her file had been transferred to Heaven! Extensive tests proved she was completely cured. Within a year the seven other people with the same illness were all dead. Katie has been well and rejoicing for more than twenty years now.

Midweek Bible study was added to the regular Sunday school in Claremont. This, combined with several fruitful tent meetings, produced a church that needed a pastor. God laid this burden on our dear friends, Hans and Lil Botes, a responsibility they fulfilled with considerable faithfulness and success for many years.

George Moore was a man with a tremendous burden for the lost. He came from California in the '30s and walked or rode a bicycle up and down South Africa proclaiming the truth of God's Word. Some seed fell on good ground—the church in Durban is the result of his ministry.

He suffered there and was imprisoned in a dank basement for several months. When he escaped, he left, hoping to return with reinforcements, but though a tragedy prevented this, his labor was not in vain. The work he started has known many storms and heartaches, but it has survived and continues with steady progress. When my mother, Carrie Eastridge, came in 1956, she was led to pastor the group. Under her leadership, they achieved stability. A hilltop church stands as a landmark today.

The churches in Sparks Estate, Durban, Claremont, and Pretoria were the small beginnings of the Colored District of the United Pentecostal Church of South Africa. Nelson Haines pastors Sparks Estate today and is the dedicated superintendent of this growing work.

"Blessed Assurance," the old hymn, had a special meaning for Bug in his early ministry and has been woven as a ribbon of hope through our adventures in Africa. The many victories recorded do not mean there were no setbacks or losses. These came with alarming regularity, but all were met with *his* song.

Let there be a financial crisis or desperate need, we would hear over and over,

Blessed assurance,
Jesus is mine! . . .

Confidence betrayed by unscrupulous men or a trusted worker who failed? He bore down on,

O what a foretaste
of glory divine! . . .

Fruitless labor or failure of an undertaking? His encouragement was,

Heir of salvation,
Purchase of God, . . .

An attack made on his personal integrity?

Born of His Spirit,
Washed in His blood.

I must confess that on-the-spot appreciation was often lacking on my part. Though tone deaf, he is still my favorite singer, so it wasn't the off-key whistling and singing that bothered me but the audacity of *any* song under those circumstances.

Finally, I realized the first glimpse of victory usually came when the chorus was repeated persistently,

"This is my story,
This is my song,
Praising my Savior
All the day long."

Then, we would see the first, faint glow of a dark tunnel's end, low places begin lifting inexplicably, and the inpregnable mountain start a surprising slide to the sea.

Eventually, doubting Thomas learned to sing along,

This is our story,
This is our song!

Bug felt led to put the tent up at Eersterust, where tribal blacks lived in a conglomerate of slum mazes. Seating arrangements were the usual five-gallon oil cans for the interpreters and us, Mother Earth for our audience, who straggled in all during service, drawn by curiosity. Lights were the standard pressure lanterns, whose variable flickerings required frequent attacks of vigorous pumping. They required mantles, and small, new packages of these were all too often the objects of serious "hide and seek" games. Bibles and my accordion completed our equipment list. I suffered a secret grief for years over my limited musical ability, but looking back, I realize my accordion noises did help draw crowds, and the case was often a rather low but handy Bible stand.

The first few services were ordinary. Then, one night, we were plunged unexpectedly into the extraordinary. When we arrived, the crowd was already there—and what a crowd! Attendance had ranged from eighty to a hundred and fifty or so before, but now our thoughtful helpers had removed the side curtains, and here were over a thousand people packed into the tent and sitting closely around the edges! We were completely baffled by the size of the crowd and their quiet air of expectancy.

"Samuel, what has happened?"

"The people have come to church, Moruti."

"I see that, Samuel, but something must have made them come. There are so many compared to last night. Do you know why?"

"It may be the little girl, sir."

"Little girl?" Bewildered, Bug looked at Samuel for further explanation. Slowly and tediously, the story came out.

Because of our strong belief that divine healing is an integral part of the Calvary package, we had made it a practice to close every service with prayer for the sick—with no fanfare or special attention drawn to what we were doing. The night before a mother had brought her deaf-mute daughter of eight for prayer. On the way home, it was discovered that the girl could both hear and speak! The word spread, and the afflicted, the hungry, and the curious turned out en masse the following night.

We began to minister in the name of Jesus with trembling realization of our utter helplessness. He did not fail! We are content to know only a few of the many miracles that took place by the power of that beautiful name. Many of the people lived in faraway places and did not return to testify, but the prayer line increased until we had prayed for several hundred nightly.

A mother brought her daughter of about thirty with the help of her sons. She was a wretched creature, obviously insane.

"Can your Jesus help my child? She has no understanding. We have kept her tied to a stake most of her life. She becomes so violent."

Bug answered that the power of Jesus was unlimited. I asked if the daughter understood English or Afrikaans (we wanted her to say "Jesus"), but she could only speak her native Sesotho, and the interpreter could not make her understand. Suddenly, she looked straight at Bug, and her voice sent chills down my spine.

"I'm not afraid of you!"

"No, Satan, but you are afraid of the One I serve," Bug answered, recognizing the speaker.

"You can't make me come out!"

"No, I can't, but Jesus can!" When Bug said "Jesus," the woman dodged as though she were slapped. He turned to all of us standing near and said, "Keep repeating 'in the name of Jesus' until deliverance comes."

The woman screamed in that awful voice, "I won't come out! I won't come out! You can't make me come out!"

Bug answered, "Satan, I refuse to argue with you. I command you in the name of Jesus to come out of this woman. You have tormented her too long!"

She fell to the ground with a loud cry. She looked lifeless, but as we knelt around her and prayed, we saw her features transformed. Soon the Holy Spirit took control, and she began to rejoice and worship the Lord in other tongues. She left the tent completely normal!

A woman badly crippled with arthritis shuffled

painfully to us one night. Her arms were knotted and stiff with minimum movement possible. She showed us how she struggled to eat and the many burn scars where she had fallen when trying to tend her cooking pots, perched over open fires. She said, "Oh, if God would just make my feet work right and my arms go up and down!"

I explained God's ability to heal and His great love, then said, "Now, when Moruti finishes his prayer for you in the name of Jesus and says 'Amen,' you must immediately start walking and lifting your arms up and down while you praise the Lord. You will be healed."

She believed with childlike simplicity and after Bug's "Amen" marched away with firm steps, swinging her arms up and down while shouting, "Hallelujah! Hallelujah! Hallelujah!"

But the next night she was in the prayer line again.

"I thought Jesus healed you last night?"

"Oh, He did! He made my feet loose and my arms go up and down. See!" she demonstrated. "But they won't go sideways. Now, if Jesus can make them go up and down, can't He make them go sideways, too?"

I showed her exactly what to do after prayer, and when Bug said "Amen," she walked away rejoicing loudly and hugging herself with crossed arms every step!

17

The God of the Black Man, Too

A hopeless sort of drama was being enacted thirty-five miles away on a farm near Bronkhorspruit. Anna Banda had been helpless for fifteen years since the birth of her son and only child. Her arms and legs were not paralyzed but limp and useless from a strange fever she contracted after childbirth.

Her husband, Abram, was a tailor and a most unusual man. Many Africans would not have stayed with an invalid wife who no longer bore the children demanded by their culture. His love for her was evident. He would work hard, save money, and take Anna on a tedious donkey cart pilgrimage to whatever witch doctor bush rumors appraised as having great magical powers.

There had been many long waits and great disappointments, but at last, they were able to visit the one who was supposed to be most powerful. He specified a completely black sheep for a sacrifice to the spirits, and after appropriate incantations and rituals, he slit the under body of the sheep from neck to tail and roughly thrust Anna's useless limbs into the carcass of the dying sheep.

He explained to Abram that Anna must lay like that

until the animal's blood was absolutely cold, then life from the sheep's body would enter her arms and legs, and they would be normal again. The theory probably sounded logical to a naive African mind. The only problem was . . . it didn't work! The witch doctor produced a white hair he claimed to have found on the animal and declared it the reason for the operation's failure. He wanted to start all over again with a truly black sheep. But Abram's money was gone, and as he washed blood and muck off his helpless wife, he plunged to a new depth of despair.

After Anna was settled on her grass mat and asleep, he slipped outside and wandered disconsolately up and down under the brilliant pageantry of the high veld starry sky. Then he remembered something he heard long ago and looking up said, "God of the white man, I have heard You live beyond the stars. If You will hear a black man's prayer, have mercy on us and heal my wife."

He felt tension drain away and turned back to the hut and his sleeping mat with a strange, unexpected peace. That night he dreamed that a man dressed in shining white stood by him.

"Abram, take your wife to Eersterust. You will find help on the east side of town."

There was a different feeling as they started on this journey. But Anna was weak, and the donkeys slow and balky, so it took three days to make the trip. He found a family of his own tribe who would care for Anna while he searched for the promised help. He was perturbed when they said the East was considered unlucky, but he had faith in his dream and started early in the morning canvassing the whole east side of the sprawling township. A witch doctor was the only thing he knew to ask for, so he questioned every person who would talk to him and heard repeatedly the same story all day long.

"There are no witch doctors on the east side—it's unlucky."

In the flaring lantern light, the crowd under and around the tent sang with fervor and enthusiasm. Abram paused on his way home to tell Anna he had failed to find help.

"But I'll try again tomorrow," he thought. He remembered seeing the outside of circus tents in Johannesburg, so he came closer and asked a bystander, "Is this a circus?"

"No, it's a strange kind of church. They don't use needles or give medicines, but they pray for sick people, and they are healed. Last night a very bent old woman crawled in here. She hadn't walked in eight years, but when they laid hands on her, she stood up straight and walked out!"

Abram's soul lifted with hope. "This is what I've been looking for. I must go and bring Anna. . . ." Then a sobering thought shook him. "Uh, what is the cost of the healing prayer?"

"Cost? There are no charges. They don't ask for money."

He left running, weariness dissolved by new hope. By the time Abram and his friends wrapped Anna in a blanket and laid her on another blanket for a stretcher and carried her to the tent, we had prayed for so many people fatigue did not allow us even to open our eyes. The workers were not very informative, saying simply, "a man" or "a woman" or "a child" as they led the seeker to us and guided our hands to lay on each head. We did not see that Anna was carried to us when we whispered the same short but heartfelt prayer we had prayed over hundreds of others.

"In the name of Jesus, be healed!" Neither did we see her a few feet away from us when she told Abram and her friends, "Put me down; there is life in my legs. I can walk!" And she did!

The next afternoon, Bug went out to tighten tent ropes and to strengthen the position of some wobbly stakes. Anna came to him shyly. Her Afrikaans and English were both limited, but she wanted to communicate and said brokenly, "Look, my hands!" She spread them out.

"Yes, I see," Bug answered politely.

"Uh . . . my feet, see?" pointing.

"Yes, you have two of each, both hands and feet," he said.

She smiled happily. "I go for water!"

"Fine, fine," he answered. By this time, Anna had decided he did not understand and went in search of an interpreter. As he explained what had happened, Bug was astounded at the extent of Anna's beautiful miracle. She must have longed so often for a drink of water and the privilege of performing her wifely duty of bringing water for her family in her years of helplessness. Her testimonies always concluded with a beaming smile, ". . . and now, I go always for water!"

Later, Abram became a preacher of the Word. He passed away after several years of fruitful ministry, but Anna is still a radiant witness to the power in the name of Jesus.

The appalling drunkenness and rowdiness of the Christmas season in such squatter areas made the close of the meetings expedient, but the last service was unforgettable. There were incredible testimonies and a whole assortment of wonder works, but I must confess that we whizzed the last few through the prayer line and tried to get them headed for home in a hurry.

Wind from an approaching storm was flapping the tent

furiously. The high veldt usually has spectacular lightning displays, but this night, the whole heavens crackled and flashed with blue-white fire, emphasized by immense, inky black, rolling clouds in the background. Dust whipped in our eyes, and the canvas billowed wildly while I helped Bug wrestle with the tent to prevent it from blowing away. Just as we ducked our heads to run for the car, a taxi squealed to a halt beside us in swirls of dust. A woman called to us, "Wait, please!" as she helped a teenage girl out of the vehicle.

"I only heard about these services today. Don't say we are too late. I have traveled fifty miles by train to bring my daughter for prayer. She has been completely deaf since a bad fall on a train four years ago. The doctors say she will never regain her hearing, but if you will pray . . ."

Bug quickly gave her a summary of as much gospel as he felt the imminent storm would allow and concluded: "The Bible says, 'faith cometh by hearing, and hearing by the word of God.' Since your daughter cannot hear, you must listen and believe for her. We will lay our hands on her in the name of Jesus, and He will open her ears . . . then you'd better run."

We prayed briefly and ran, but the storm's fury caught us before we gained the safety of the car.

A few weeks later, the same mother knocked on our door. "I suppose the storm made you hurry that night. You only prayed for one ear! My daughter hears perfectly with the right ear, so we have come for prayer for the other one that is still deaf."

Bug was perplexed until he noticed Agnes, our house help, listening intently. Then he realized why this had happened. Agnes was very skeptical. When we witnessed to her, she insisted, "Oh, yes, Jesus loves white people and will heal them, but He won't do anything for black people." Nothing we could say would change her mind.

Bug answered the lady, "I have a couple of urgent letters to write; you visit with Agnes for a while, and I'll pray for your daughter later." He disappeared into his office. When he was sure the story of the healed ear had been repeated several times, he returned and said, "Now, I am ready to pray for the left ear."

He did, and healing was an instant fact. It was comical to watch Agnes test the girl's hearing in both ears every way she could think of. When the lady and her daughter went on their way rejoicing, Agnes came to us and said, "I have seen, and now I believe!"

The African church born of this endeavor was later moved to a new location with a beautiful name, Mamolodi. The slums were bulldozed, new houses built, and Eersterust became the home of the people who formerly lived in Claremont and other squatter villages. Under the wise guidance of Hans and Lil Botes, the church made a progressive transition. Many willing hands helped build a remarkable church that stands there today—a corner soul-saving station.

When failing health retired the faithful leaders, Sammy Linton, one of my original Sunday school pupils, became pastor. Now, the growing church in Eersterust is ably pastored by a small, dedicated man named James Oliphant.

18

The Foreboding Dream

Mother's church-building program in Sparks Estate, Durban, was in serious financial difficulty in 1957. Several other situations also needed Bug's word of wisdom. We were flown down by a friend, Stewart Stucki, in his four-seater Fairchild. His wife kept our children at their small farm three miles from Pretoria. In Durban there were consultations, a few services, and some temporary financial relief found. But since the European church in Pretoria was just getting started, we felt it imperative to return for the Sunday services.

Long before the alarm clock rang early that Sunday morning, I was awake and very troubled by a strange dream. I dreamed a huge snake crawled on the bed between us and spit first in my face and then in Bug's. Bug felt this was a warning, so we prayed together for God's mercy and guidance. The day was beautiful, but even as I admired the crisp morning topped with fantasies of luminous pink and white cloud formations, I felt the dark edge of *something* ahead.

The air journey shortened the four hundred road miles considerably. We had arranged that Sandra, 18, Dale 16, and Sally Stucki, 17, would go early to our home, where services were held, to prepare for Sunday school and start the service if we were late. When we landed at the small airport nearby we phoned for Fred (Stucki's son) to come to get us. Anna Stucki said the young people had left about an hour before. When we reached the house, Anna was frantic—someone had just phoned that our children were involved in a serious accident. We must go to the hospital at once!

On the way we passed the gray car our children had driven. We didn't stop. Apparently it had sideswiped one tree on a curve and crashed head-on into another one. Considering the appearance of the car, we couldn't help but wonder fearfully what we would find at the hospital. We prayed all the way.

Dale met us at the door with some evident bruises, shaken and pale. "I'm OK, Mom and Dad—Sally's face is badly cut, but Sandra's really hurt."

There were tears in his eyes as he led us to the emergency room where Sandra lay on a stretcher, broken glass in her hair and blood splattered all over her white dress. Six doctors and our friend, Dr. Kessell, examined her alternately. She had a crushed skull, deeply lacerated leg, and symptoms of serious internal injuries, besides minor cuts and abrasions. The doctors agreed that she could not live but wanted to do exploratory surgery to determine the extent of her injuries. We asked if the operation they proposed could save her life. The answer was, "No hope," so we refused to give our permission for surgery.

While nurses transferred Sandra to a room, we went to see Sally. A doctor was trying to stitch her face back together. Her nose was almost cut off. Somehow, injections were ineffectual against the excruciating pain, and both

Sally and the doctor were unnerved by her anguish. I held her hands and prayed while the doctor did the delicate stitching that left her with minimal scars later.

The nurses were afraid to move Sandra enough to change her clothes. We sat by her bed the rest of the day and could hear the broken bones of her head grating together as she tossed in delirium. She fretted over the Sunday school and called pitifully, "Mother, Mother," over and over without hearing my answer. There was nothing to do but wait and ache and pray. When night approached, Bug said, "I feel I should go home for the night service, honey."

"I'll go, too," I answered. "If ever I needed a service, it's now."

The nurse in charge promised to phone us if there was any change in her condition. The doctor recommended that we go home and made it clear it was only a matter of time.

While I was combing my hair, the phone rang, a casual friend asked, "How did this accident happen?"

"It appears a tubeless tire was nearly flat, no one noticed, and it snapped off in the curve just as the car was accelerated to make the hill."

She interrupted, "What I really want to know is *Why?* We drove out and looked at the car; it's a wreck! We went to the hospital to see Sandra and I don't believe she will live through the night. How could God let such a thing happen?"

"I don't understand *why*," I answered, "but I must trust the Lord. I have purposed in my heart not to question Him."

"It doesn't make sense," the irate voice continued. "The car bought for you by churches in America for the work of the Lord in Africa is totaled! Sandra is dying—such a con-secrated girl, a good example to all of us, besides being your faithful helper with the music and Sunday school. I want to know why! There must be a reason!"

The caller did not realize that her words were like twisting a knife in a fresh, raw wound. I silently prayed for wisdom.

"I'm content to leave it all in God's hands, and I will not ask why, but if He lets me know a reason, I'll phone you." I hung up.

There wasn't time for a long prayer meeting, but I whispered, "Lord, I'm not asking why or wherefore for myself, but if a reason or explanation will help this lady, please speak to me."

I reached for my Bible, and it fell open at Matthew Seven—the account of two houses. The phone was on a low table near where I knelt, and I quickly dialed my friend.

"I've received an answer for you from the Lord. God does not wrap His children in a protective shield and put them on a shelf away from danger and the realities of life. It's all in the story of two houses. Let me read it to you. It's in Matthew 7:24-27.

> *Therefore whosoever heareth these sayings of mine, and doeth them, I will liken him unto a wise man, which built his house upon a rock: And the rain descended, and the floods came, and the winds blew, and beat upon that house; and it fell not: for it was founded upon a rock. And every one that heareth these sayings of mine, and doeth them not, shall be likened unto a foolish man, which built his house upon the sand: And the rain descended, and the floods came, and the winds blew, and beat upon that house; and it fell: and great was the fall of it.*

"Don't you see? Both houses had the same storms. This proves God's fairness. Troubles, cancer, tragedies and accidents happen to God's children as well as to those who do not serve Him. Our heads are bowed now in the face of a storm. If Sandra dies, it will be like having both arms chopped off—the hardest thing I've ever faced—but my house will stand because by His grace I have built on the rock."

I went downstairs to the service with unexpected strength to take Sandra's place at the piano, something I had dreaded doing.

When Bug phoned the hospital after church, her condition was unchanged. We were requested not to come; the doctor advised that we rest and promised again to call us if there was any deterioration.

The other children went home with friends. We lay wide-eyed in the still, dark house, emotionally and physically exhausted. Neither of us spoke. The clock downstairs started striking midnight—the sound seemed abnormally loud. I automatically counted the "dongs," and on the twelfth one, the chilling knowledge gripped me. "Sandra is dying now." As I fell out of bed on my knees, I realized Bug did the same on the other side of the bed. Then I thought, if it is God's will to take my child, I don't want to be guilty of resisting Him or begging for her life against His will. So in my heart I lifted her up in my arms to Jesus and prayed only for His will to be done. An exquisite sense of God's presence and a pervading peace filled the room; we were completely still in His nearness. Then Bug came and lifted me from the floor.

"Our girl was nearly gone, honey, but God has spared her for us. Let us praise Him!" And we did.

The phone rang repeatedly from very early the next morning. Most of the conversations were the same.

"How's Sandra?"

"She's better."

"Does the doctor think there is hope?"

"Oh, we haven't heard from the doctor yet, but we have heard from heaven. She is going to be all right!"

I waited for Anna, and together, we went to see our daughters. Sally's bruised face was mottled blue and swollen, but she was cheerful. Sandra was pale and weak but fully conscious. I was thankful for a gown in place of that sad-looking white dress. I went to the nurse, "Why weren't we called when Sandra took the bad turn at midnight?"

She looked startled. "Who told you?"

"Never mind, I *know!* Now, I want you to tell me exactly what happened."

"She started slipping away suddenly," she answered. "There wasn't time to call you. Two doctors and six nurses worked with her trying everything they knew, including oxygen. Finally, one doctor said, 'It's no use. She's gone!' He directed a strong flashlight beam in her eyes, and there was no reaction. A nurse held a mirror to her mouth—there was no breath and no pulse. Just as they turned away, thinking it was all over, she sighed and started breathing again and regained consciousness soon afterward. She is miraculously on the way to recovery, beyond everyone's expectation."

Incredibly, she was discharged from the hospital five days later with only the stipulation that she should rest for two weeks.

Sandra had been so nearsighted her vision blurred at twelve inches. She had worn glasses from her early teens, and since they were broken in the wreck, she asked her second day in the hospital for us to get her a new pair so she could read. But on my next visit, I found her reading without them.

"Mother, I can't wear these glasses. I can see better without them."

After she left the hospital and was able, we took her for a thorough eye examination. The doctor was puzzled with the results.

"I can't understand how she ever endured these glasses. This girl's eyes are normal; she doesn't need glasses at all."

"May I ask a question, Doctor? If a person had faulty eyesight and suffered severe concussion through an accident, could this have a beneficial effect on one's vision?"

"Absolutely not, Mrs. Freeman. Concussion could only have an adverse effect on the faculty of sight."

Later, I asked the same question of the hospital specialist in charge of Sandra's case and received the same answer. The gift of life and healing was accompanied by several extraordinary benefits.

The auto insurance paid promptly with almost the exact amount long overdue on the church construction in Durban. God has His own ways to answer prayer.

There was a small glimpse into matters that are little understood. In the second week of her convalescence, Sandra asked me to sit with her awhile one afternoon. She wanted to talk.

"Mother, there is something very puzzling. After the accident I was oblivious to everything but pain. I felt I was in a vise of terrible pain that was closing in on me, and it seemed unending.

"Then, the strangest thing happened. I realized I was in

a hospital, but I was detached from everything. I looked down on myself lying on a bed. There were two doctors and five or six nurses working with the Sandra on the bed. They tried to give her oxygen. I heard one of the doctors say, 'It's no use. She's gone.' Then he shined a flashlight into her eyes, and one of the nurses held a mirror to her mouth and said, 'There is no breath.' Another one said, 'No pulse.' It was as though there were two of me—that still Sandra on the bed and myself watching. A lovely light glowed around me, and I thought with joy, 'The pain is gone, and now, I will go live with Jesus.' But the next thing I knew, I was back in that hurting body. Not long after that, I became conscious of my surroundings and was able to talk to the nurses and the doctor. What does it all mean, Mother? Was I that near to death?"

I was too deeply moved to say anything for several moments. There was no way she could have known the nurse's description of that midnight crisis, yet the accounts matched precisely. I held her close.

"I'm not sure I understand all of it, honey, but I do know you were nearly gone and God spared you for us. We will be forever grateful."

The next development was a budding romance between Sandra and Fred Stucki.

19

A Gift Bird

The natural sequence of children maturing and leaving home is hard on parents. We realize the inevitable will come, but we are never quite prepared for it to happen. The separation is even more drastic for missionaries because of distances and prescribed term length. The trauma is often deepened by circumstances that shove fledglings from the parental nest when they are still so young and vulnerable.

Our turn was near in the beginning of 1958. Dale's education plans would prevent his returning with us after furlough. Sandra was dreaming of wedding bells. Home would not be the same again, and I grasped every tiny memory to cherish against the longing, lonely times ahead. Only loving-kindness could have provided this small, delightful remembrance of the last month we were all together.

If our windows were screened or if there had been lace or net to obscure the view, it couldn't have happened. "Getting up time" arrived with its usual punctuality that early morning, but I was still praying for grace to meet the day and trying to survey a route through all that should be done when we were startled by sudden tapping on our window. We sat up quickly. A large bird with vivid plumage eyed us with a friendly glint while he alternated delicate taps with his beak on the solid, center window pane with a hopping ballet on the wide sill. He had wings of black that silvered into metallic gray, edged with white, a jaunty crest, and a flamboyant yellow, shaded breast. He continued his bell-toned rhythm until both of us were up and moving, then he flew away with an air of, "My, but you are slow today."

Lynda grumbled at breakfast, "That dumb bird wouldn't stop pecking on my window until I got up!" When we compared reports, we discovered that every bedroom had been visited! We assumed this was a remarkable onetime experience, but not so—our self-appointed herald was there every morning, cheerfully tapping out a wake-up call *in the order of age.*

This was the most amazing part. He began his routine at our northwest bedroom, then flew to the opposite northeast corner to waken Sandra. Next in line was Dale in the middle room on the south, then the adjoining southeast corner to let Lynda know it was time to rise and shine. When everyone else was up, he doubled back to the middle north-facing room occupied by our two youngest daughters, Sharon and Marla. I had never known my clan to be so wide awake and alert at *that* hour of the morning. A few abortive attempts were made to lay hold on Mr. Yellow Breast—but mostly he was regarded as a special friend.

About a month afterwards, Bug, Sandra, and Dale left by air for the States, and we did not see or hear from our feathered alarm clock again. The three youngest girls and I went later by boat. Still today, at any family get-together, someone will say, "Dad, remember that bird . . . ?" Divine wisdom bestows not only large mercies but lighthearted memories to grace tedious times.

20
"Some" Traveling

By 1969 the work had expanded to require almost constant supervisory travel. Often the eighteen-foot travel trailer was our diminutive haven as we swung through itineraries that could range anywhere from five hundred to three thousand miles. Our stops varied from brief, first-time visits with new contacts to a day or so with established churches. At times the trailer stayed home, but *always* we went.

In May of that year, we embarked on a short tour, planning to touch a dozen or so points. Our first stop was Klerksdorp. Though the weather was cold, I was warmly dressed, so I could not understand why I shivered all through the evening service. By the time we reached the pastor's home afterward, I was racked by attacks of violent coughing. Then in the night, the fever came. It was evident that the planned trip could not continue, so Bug made a bed for me in the back seat, and we started home.

On the way, we made a brief stop at the home of a woman who wanted to be baptized. She had been introduced to Jesus Name baptism through a *Harvestime* broadcast. Upon our arrival, she sympathized with my condition and agreed to wait until a more convenient time. Just before we left, she looked in the window of the car and exclaimed: "Reverend Freeman, take your wife to the hospital at once—she is desperately ill!"

Because of an extreme allergy to any type of drug or medication, my only alternatives are prayer and rest. But when six weeks had elapsed and neither had prevailed, Bug decided to call our friend, Dr. Kessell. His verdict was severe Asiatic flu—complicated by double pneumonia and my twice getting out of bed prematurely. The prescription was six *more* weeks of complete bed rest. I *thought* I was as miserable as could be with that dreary prospect, then the phone rang.

A respected friend spoke: "Sister Freeman, I really don't know how to tell you this, but I feel I must. The entire church has been fasting and praying for your healing—with no results. For the past three days, I have been fasting, asking the Lord to show me why the church was unable to gain the victory. He has . . ." There was a long pause.

"Yes . . . tell me, please," I pled.

"Well, I don't understand, but . . . th . . . the Lord said your consecration has slipped."

I mumbled my thanks and said "Good-bye." This indictment might have been quickly dismissed if the caller were a frivolous and unspiritual person, but the very opposite was true. I felt as though the whole world had caved in on me. In feverish misery and weakness, I tried in vain to pray and search my heart the remainder of the day. For the life of me, I could not think of a single consecration I had ever made that I had allowed to slip. Dark heaviness enveloped my room, and sleep evaded me for hours.

The vision came shortly before dawn. It seemed the

Savior was sitting in a chair by the bed that had been my prison for so long. I couldn't see Him, but I knew He was there just the same.

"O Jesus, I'm so glad You are here—my heart is troubled. My sister says my consecration has slipped, and it must be so, but I don't know where or what. Please tell me."

"Yes," He answered, "your consecration to travel for Me has changed."

"Travel? I don't understand—we go all the time." I was perplexed.

"Yes, you go but with complaints and dissatisfaction."

"But, Lord, I don't remember complaining."

"Have you forgotten that I see your heart? I know your attitude. Bug says to get ready for a trip, and while you are packing the suitcases, you are thinking, 'I get so tired packing and unpacking. Must we always go, go, go?' I'm not able to use you as I desire wherever you go, for your thoughts are continually on returning home. You are either counting your days or the miles. I am not pleased with such service. If you wish to hear My 'Well done,' you must do all things with a willing heart. Work or go gladly with praises to Me in your heart as well as on your lips."

"Oh, forgive me, dear Friend; I didn't realize what I was doing. Help me give true service to You and to always be thankful."

Then came precious words I will never forget: "You are forgiven, and I *will* help you, but if it is My will for you to live out of suitcases for the rest of your life, let it be with a glad, willing heart."

My first deep, restful sleep in many weeks followed this meeting. At 9:30 A.M. Bug woke me to say the ladies of the church had come for a prayer meeting. When they prayed for me, I was instantly healed.

Bug insisted that Dr. Kessell confirm the healing before he would allow me to get up. So twenty-four hours after the good doctor's initial verdict, he said, "Hmmm, they must have prayed the prayer of faith for you. Your lungs are clear, and you can get out of bed. Just promise me you will rest some each day until you completely regain your strength."

Later, when I shared my visitation from God with Bug, I said, "If we are to go more than we have in the past, we're gonna have to do *some* traveling!" With this he smiled and gave me a hug.

"I'm so glad the Lord has prepared you," Bug assured me. I wondered what he meant but didn't ask. Two years later, in 1971, Bug was appointed Regional Field Supervisor for the entire continent of Africa, and ever since then we have done *some* traveling.

21
Tragedy Hits

Easter is conference time in South Africa. One night in 1973 is indelibly stamped on my memory. Sandra was playing the organ, and the choir's singing was heavenly as Bug leaned close to me. "Nona, I don't want to alarm you, but I feel I should share with you a warning from the Lord about the trip ahead of us. There will be a problem."

In my mind I quickly reviewed our plans. Kenneth Phillips was preaching this conference and would leave with us immediately afterwards for a crusade in Ghana. Our next stop was in Nigeria for a conference, then on to the Cameroons, where a precarious situation had developed (maybe *that* was where the problem waited for us?). Next was Kenya and Madagascar.

"Do you know where?" I softly asked.

His whispered answer came. "Yes, Kenya. Now you are not to worry, but we do need to pray about it."

The crusade in Accra, Ghana, was like the Book of Acts happening all over again. Gerald Mangun from Alexandria, Louisiana, joined us after visiting Kenya, the Cameroons, and Nigeria. Only heaven has an accurate record of all the miracles and answered prayers. We do know that a kid-napped baby was returned to her mother, the lame walked, the blind saw, the deaf heard, and those pitifully bound by demons and witchcraft were released. The greatest joy of all was witnessing over nine hundred filled with the baptism of the Holy Spirit. There were probably many more unnoticed among the masses who responded to the altar invitations in the ten days of services.

Midway, a letter came from Bill Cupples, missionary to Kenya, asking Bug to go with him and Missionary John Harris to dedicate a new church building at Bukolo, near Lake Victoria. Bug tossed the letter to me and said casually, almost as though he spoke to himself, "That trip will end in tragedy."

I answered excitedly, "Then you mustn't go! If you think this trip will end in tragedy, call it off. You can refuse to go, you know."

He answered calmly, "I didn't mean to say 'tragedy'—that's probably too strong a word. I'll pray about whether or not to go. I'm sure the Lord will lead me right."

The next day, Bug said, "Honey, I don't know about that trip. I'm concerned about going, but I keep feeling it's the will of the Lord. Help me pray about it."

"Just one more night of the crusade!" I thought as we reached the hotel, weary from the day's activities and a long, beautiful evening service in tropical humidity. The neat twin beds looked inviting. Bug got ready for his quickly and was asleep the moment his head hit the pillow. A few minutes after midnight, I turned off my bedside lamp, but as my head touched the pillow, I was gripped by a sudden need to pray and immediately rolled from the bed to my knees. One learns something of travailing prayer when walking with Jesus, but I cannot remember a burden taking me with such urgency before.

Tears flowed as I pled for mercy and deliverance and grace. There was no indication of what or for whom I prayed. I knew, however, that it was a matter of life and death—that I wrestled with encroaching darkness and serious dangers that were ahead. Then suddenly, as it had come, the load lifted and I felt the sweet release of peace. I glanced at my watch—it was 2:00 A.M.

But again, just as I stretched out on the bed, I was seized with a burden even more compelling than the first one. In my first prayer, I was conscious of being in a hotel and knew the wisdom of praying quietly. But now I groaned and agonized with a travail of spirit that made me completely uncaring as to whether or not I disturbed everyone in the hotel. I lay full length on the floor and felt the crushing weight of evil as I wrestled with forces beyond my comprehension. It seemed I was losing the battle when I remembered the words of Romans 8:26:

> *Likewise the Spirit also helpeth our infirmities: for we know not what we should pray for as we ought: but the Spirit itself maketh intercession for us with groanings which cannot be uttered.*

I cried to the Lord for His Spirit to help and make intercession for me, and He did. This time the victory came slowly; by degrees I felt the darkness recede. When the "peace of overcoming" rolled over me, I stood up—it was 5:00 A.M.

With the thought of getting some rest, I fell in the bed. For the third time, I was struck with a burden. On my knees

I asked for strength to pray through this one, too, and began requesting deliverance and help as before. I became conscious of a still, small voice saying "No."

"Please, Lord," I begged. "Give me this victory, also."

Again, that gentle "No." Seven times I heard it—as a wise father, knowing what is best for his beloved child, must reluctantly deny a request. I could do nothing more than bow in submission. "Thy will be done."

When Bug awoke at 6:00 A.M., he found me wide-eyed.

"My, but you are awake early!" He was surprised because I'm not an early bird. I told him I had not slept at all and why. Neither of us could understand it—nor did we think of my night of prayer in connection with the warning.

There was much to enjoy in Nigeria—fellowship with the H. E. Gerald missionary family and services in jungle churches. One of these services was made unusual by a stocky African man with a length of loincloth around his waist (in lieu of pants) who was so deeply moved by the Spirit he was oblivious to everything around him. He gave a message in tongues and interpreted in his native dialect, which we couldn't understand. We missed a lot of it before an older minister said excitedly, "Wait! Wait, this message is for you," and began to translate sketchily into English. The gist was a warning of trouble and danger, softened by a promise that the Lord's presence would be there and that He is the Conqueror. We still thought the promise was for people present whom we knew were apprehensive about the future.

After the service, I again suggested that Bug cancel the trip to Kenya. It was causing him so much concern.

"No," he answered, "I can't because I feel it's God's will to go."

The Cameroons were depressing because of restrictions that hindered the work. It was evident that the Basil Williams missionary family would be forced to leave shortly. Together, we tried to muster faith that the doors would open.

Before we left Douala, at midnight on May 20, I asked Bug for the third time to reconsider his decision about *the* trip.

He answered, "What kind of soldier for the Lord would I be if I refused to do my duty for fear I would be hurt? Whatever happens on that journey is God's will, dear—I guess that's that."

The night flight on Air Ethiopia is a good one, and we really needed sleep. But in spite of extreme weariness, I was miserably cold and unable to relax. The stewardesses were kind and kept bringing blankets and hot tea, but the chill started in my heart, and nothing helped. My legs ached, and I hoped to get off and walk a bit at Entebbe, but we were not allowed to disembark. I closed my eyes and whispered over and over, "Help us, Lord, help us," while I shivered the rest of the night. Bug did not sleep either.

We crossed two time zones and arrived in Nairobi at 7:30 A.M. Bill Cupples, a most exuberant missionary, met us.

"Say, Brother Bug, I'm so glad you stopped me that day at World Evangelism Center and talked to me about Kenya. I've never been so happy in my life nor so sure I'm in the exact will of God. I've had a privilege few of my buddies have ever known—I baptized sixteen trinitarian preachers in the name of Jesus in *one* afternoon! Remember how you helped us house hunting when you were here before, Sister Freeman? Well, we found that special house and moved in three weeks ago today."

The house was lovely, set in spacious grounds. We were glad for them. We visited with the Cupples and Harris families and at noon enjoyed delicious "Irish stew" Cupples style.

Bill explained, "I told Frances a person never knows when an emergency will come. I've made two big pressure pots full of stew for the freezer. I'm sure it will come in handy."

We stood by the car and prayed together before the three men left about 1:00 P.M. Jerri remembered John's dreaming the previous night that their son Jonathan was killed by a truck, so she called as the car moved slowly away, "You fellows watch out for the big trucks on that road!"

I felt like I was in a vacuum, waiting for an unknown axe to fall. Even my own voice sounded strange in my ears.

Frances said, "You look so tired. Why don't you rest awhile?" I went to my room and tried to read a book on the Blue Nile, but my eyes refused to focus. Finally, I dozed only to awaken with a sudden, heart-wrenching panic. I prayed until I felt calm, then wandered into the living room and sat holding a newspaper in front of me—only realizing later it was upside down. The afternoon dragged by.

Shortly after 5:00 P.M., thirteen-year-old Eddie Cupples yelled, "Visitors!" Frances saw from the kitchen window and called to me.

"Jerri has brought the Kirbys to see you." Richard and Ila Kirby were our first friends in Kenya. But when they entered the room, I saw by their faces that the axe had fallen. Jerri and Ila fell, one on each shoulder, talking incoherently.

Jerri said over and over, "They didn't make it—they didn't make it!"

"Who, Jerri? Who didn't make it?"

"Bill didn't make it!"

"John?" I asked.

"Hurt!"

"Brother Freeman?" she sobbed so wildly that I barely heard . . . "Cut to pieces."

I knew I must get to Frances, but I couldn't get away from the two holding me. She came from the kitchen and greeted them with a saying common to the part of the states she came from, but it had a devastating effect on Richard.

"You folks look like you've brought a death message!" Then she saw how pale and troubled he was.

"Richard, is something wrong?"

"Yes, there's been an accident, and your husband is dead."

Eddie walked through the door in time to hear the awful news given by a man in such shock he wasn't able to cushion the blow at all. He didn't know any details. John had phoned the message briefly from the Molo police station. "Bill is dead, I'm hurt, and Brother Freeman is cut to pieces. The police are taking us to the hospital at Nakuru."

Our friends offered to drive Jerri or me to Nakuru, a hundred treacherous miles away. I knew if Bug could advise me, he would say "Your duty is to stay with Frances." So I ignored my pleading heart.

"Jerri, go with the Kirbys to see about our men, and please let me know as soon as you can."

Sonya, a Jewish friend of Frances, and her husband came, and for the next two hours we made overseas phone calls and tried in vain to find words or means to comfort the bereaved.

The lashing hurt finally eased into aching grief, and the house was still. I glanced at my watch as I waited for another call to come through. Eight o'clock. O God! I can't hear from Nakuru before midnight. How can I endure four more hours of uncertainty? Suddenly, the full impact of my share of this tragedy hit me. I began to tremble, and my legs felt as though they had turned to water. I wondered if they would ever support me again as I collapsed into a chair.

"O Jesus, if I ever needed you, I need you now." I wanted to pray for Bug but realized a pitfall was near.

"Lord, help me in this dark hour not to question anything that has happened or will happen. Deliver me from 'WHYS'—in the name of Jesus."

Then I wondered aloud, "Is Bug's work done?" If his work was done and this was the Lord's time to take him home, I didn't want to resist God's will. I never thought of my wondering as *prayer*, but I received an instant answer.

"No! His work is not done. He will still travel thousands of miles through Africa. By his efforts, new areas and countries will be opened to the gospel, and there will be a great harvest of souls. Many will pray for him and for all of you involved in this heartache—but you must NOT pray. You are to praise and thank me for *everything*! And there will be victory!"

My human reaction was, "That can't be right!" But Jesus put a portion of scripture before me as a billboard by the highway:

"GIVING THANKS ALWAYS FOR ALL THINGS . . ." (Ephesians 5:20).

With tears pouring down my face, I immediately started offering the sacrifice of praise, thanking God for the accident and everything connected with it. The hardest thing to say was, "Thank you, dear Friend, for my loved one who is cut to pieces."

I was strengthened by the praises, but it was still a long time until after midnight when Richard phoned.

"We can hope Brother Freeman will make it; he is badly cut, but they're getting ready to operate. . . ."

"Thanks so much for letting me know, Richard. But there's no doubt that my husband will make it."

"If you could see him, you might not say that."

I could hear tears in our friend's voice on the other end of the line.

"If I could see him, it might be more difficult to look at his condition and say he'll make it, but I'd still have to say it, for I've heard from heaven and I know it is so!"

He was evasive about the extent of Bug's injuries, but hearing myself state "he will make it" helped me.

Earlier, when I had phoned our Missions Headquarters in the States, Don Fisher had offered to notify our families. Frances' daughter, Ruth Ann, phoned at 2:30 A.M. and her sister at 3:00 A.M. Kenneth Phillips called at 5:00 A.M. and offered to come if it would be helpful. The willingness warmed our hearts, but prayer was our most urgent need.

In the early morning hours the following day, I realized my Friend had revealed the only route of "survival with equanimity" possible through the trial we were in. Obedience to the command to worship (as hard as it was) paid amazing dividends of cleared mind, renewed strength, and assured direction. When a new fear or anxiety threatened to overwhelm me, I learned to subdue it by thanking God FOR it.

Our mission in Kenya was comparatively new. The Harrises had been there a year and the Cupples for only seven months. I couldn't help thinking that if this accident could have been in a country where the church was well known, there would be many friends to help us. . . .

I met that thought with, "Thank you, Jesus, that this has happened in a country where we are unknown!" The Lord responded by sending friends from different directions unexpectedly and raising up new ones who stood by us faithfully.

In the night, Frances said, "Bill was my call to Africa—now, he is gone. I want to go home and take his body with me. How soon do you think we can leave?"

I answered, "We'll try for Saturday; that gives us four days." I knew it would take several miracles if this were accomplished, but I began to work on it by thanking God for the impossibility. I confess to feeling as though I were being forced to climb a perilous stairway in the dark with no handholds. But the Spirit whispered,

"One step at a time *with* praise!"

22

Blow by Blow

Halfway through the previous chapter and trying to plan this one, I was baffled. I wanted to record dates, places, and events accurately, but having a colander memory is a definite handicap.

I sent an urgent SOS signal to my Friend. I don't know what I expected—writing in the sky or an intuitive flash that would show past happenings as a computer readout—but the answer came in a most ordinary way. I felt an urge to open a certain desk drawer. "I know what's in there," I thought. Odd bits of paper and notebooks with varied scribblings and a whole collection of diary beginnings that usually expired in February.

I picked up a black-covered shorthand tablet that looked unfamiliar. The first page read January 1, 1973— how long did this one last? I flipped through the pages. Oh joy, it ended June 10. I turned back to the month of May, and there was all the needed information! Some of it was skimpy and written under such stress I could hardly read the scrawl, but the diary I didn't remember keeping at all has provided the facts—to the glory of God. The rest of the story comes from our collective memories.

May 21st, Monday

The men stopped for gas at Nakuru, a hundred miles from Nairobi. Bill said, "If you will drive, John—I think I'll get in the back seat and rest awhile."

John drove carefully since the tarred road was wet and slick in places from intermittent showers. Bug and John sat in the front seat, discussing the progress and complications of the mission in Ethiopia, when eighteen miles out of Nakuru they came upon a slow-moving dump truck that stopped in front of them on a long upgrade. The road was clear ahead, but just as John swung out to go by, a large truck suddenly appeared, careening from side to side on the narrow mountain pass road. Steering wheels are on the right and traffic moves left in Kenya. There was time to return to the left lane in front of the stopped vehicle, but John felt he wanted more distance between their car and the obviously out-of-control truck. So he accelerated off the road as far as possible to the right off the highway. The story that follows is history.

The truck crashed into the left side of the Peugeot 504. The collision took place over twenty-two feet from the road. Bill had gone to sleep with his head resting against the back left door and must have awakened immediately in the presence of the King. Bug probably threw up his left arm to shield his face. The outer shell of the two doors was ripped off, and the car whirled around 180 degrees upon impact. The truck hurtled on for several yards before coming to rest with the cab sheared from the front axle.

John was momentarily stunned, but when his mind cleared, he glanced back at Bill, calling his name. No answer. He looked closer; there was extraordinary peace, almost a glow on his face. He thought, "I guess he's knocked out."

Coming around the car to see about Bug, who was hanging halfway out, he heard him speaking and called, "Brother Freeman, are you all right?" On receiving no reply, he bent closer.

Though unconscious, Bug was talking to his Friend in a calm voice. "Jesus, You are such a precious Friend. Thank You for being so loving and merciful. I love You, Jesus. I know You are with me and will never forsake me."

Bug's left ear hung by a bit of cartilage and skin. Blood poured from numerous cuts on his head, face, and arm and gushed from a deep gash that almost severed his left arm from his body. Since he couldn't get him out, John propped him upright in the car, using Bug's beige jacket and a pillow. He noted that some road workers had gone to the aid of the man in the truck's cab. An awful loneliness overwhelmed him as he waited for help to come.

Several vehicles passed without stopping. Superstition about death and bloodshed probably hastened them on by. Eventually, police from the Molo station came by in a Landrover and stopped. They decided to take Bug and the badly injured truck driver to Molo. Other cars stopped—an English lady gave John a much appreciated cup of coffee from a thermos.

While he was helping load Bug into the back of the Landrover, an Indian man tapped John on the shoulder. "Say, did you know your friend in the back seat is dead?"

Shock on shock! He had not known. Everyone left, and there was another lonely vigil by the car where Bill Cupples lay until the police returned. The accident happened about 3:00 P.M. John reached the Molo station just before 5:00 P.M.

The truck driver was dead on arrival. From there John phoned Richard.

There is a first aid clinic attached to the police station, and a technician started stitching Bug's ear at once, without benefit of anesthesia. His first awareness was of intensified pain.

"Man, what are you doing to me?"

"I'm sewing your ear back on," replied the technician nonchalantly. Merciful unconsciousness returned for the duration of that ordeal. From then on, however, he was aware of his surroundings for longer intervals. In one lucid moment, he heard John's voice and called him, "Are you hurt? What about Bill?"

When he heard the answers, big tears rolled down Bug's cheeks.

Later, there was a wild ride in another Landrover with a drunken driver on a rough "shortcut" to the hospital at Nakuru.

Jerri reached the hospital before the doctor did. She saw the exhausted man lay his head on the desk and sleep awhile before he dared attempt the necessary surgery.

Two years later, Donald Ikerd and John met the Irish nurse who assisted with the operation. She said the doctor was making preparations to finish what the accident had partially done.

She pled, "Oh, Doctor Malakooti, don't amputate his arm. This man is a minister of the gospel."

"But this arm will be useless."

"A useless arm will be better than *no* arm!"

"I don't know if it will be possible to save it—crushed elbow and wrist, and so many lacerations. Worst of all, the arm was dragged on the ground, and the wounds are full of dirt, broken glass, and dry grass."

"Try, Doctor, please try!"

He tried and somehow put it back together. My debt of gratitude includes Dr. Malakooti, that perceptive nurse, and the many friends who waited through the tedious hours until the surgery was over and Bug was back in his room.

May 22nd, Tuesday

When I phoned our son-in-law, Brian Orffer, in Pretoria at 7:00 A.M., his mother, Molly, answered. The children were out of town, but she would contact them, our daughter, Sandra, and the Mack Carpenters. An hour later Mack called with an offer to come. Though sincerely appreciative, I felt there was only one practical answer—"Just pray for us."

Richard slept an hour and then came to Nairobi to take Jerri and me to the hospital. The road stretched ahead of us like a rough-edged, unending black ribbon. When we eventually arrived, Bug looked bad—blue, blue eyes in a waxy face with a large lump on the side of his head. I was thankful to find him fully conscious, but his left ear looked somewhat like a huge, grubby potato. The left shoulder and arm were in a cast, the right arm immobilized by an IV, and numerous superficial cuts crisscrossed his face.

"The worst of it is, I can't scratch my nose. Do the honors for me, please," he whispered.

I gently rubbed his nose.

"Bug, please let me stay with you."

"Oh, no, Frances needs you. Help her get off—do everything you can for her. I'm all right."

He looked anything but "all right," and holding to the foot of that hospital bed and praising God were the hardest hurdles yet.

One great consolation—John insisted on going home with us, against the doctor's objections that he was not able to leave the hospital. So comforting to have one of the men with us in Nairobi, even if he was suffering from severe concussion, whiplash, a huge gash on his head, and a blood clot running the whole length of one rib.

I noticed Bug's arm was set in a slightly bent position, presupposing that the arm would be useless. Remembering the Lord had promised victory, I whispered, "Thank you Lord for this problem, too."

The Persian surgeon wanted me to come to his office.

"I am concerned about your husband—he has lost so much blood I don't know if he will make it or not." There was a long pause while he looked out the window, then he turned back to me.

"In fact, I don't know how he reached the hospital alive. I had been to Tanzania and wasn't here when they brought him in. By the time they reached me via shortwave and I started the operation, more than nine hours had passed since he was injured. The time lost, excessive bleeding from multiple contaminated lacerations, *plus* the fact that we cannot give him blood transfusions build almost insurmountable odds against his recovery."

Before I could ask why transfusions could not be given, he explained.

"Kenya has had epidemics of hepatitis and malaria, and there is no clean blood available." He stood up from his desk, indicating the end of the interview. I thanked him for doing his best and left his office, silently praising my Friend.

This was the second day of the emergency that Bill Cupples foresaw, and all there was to eat after our return from Nakuru was the stew he had made and frozen. The first few bites wouldn't stay down, but then I lectured myself. "If God in His wisdom has prepared food ahead of time for these days of sorrow and pressure, *you* must eat with thanksgiving and without recrimination."

Bill's stew that sustained us the rest of the week was really as miraculous as Elijah's bread and meat that came by airmail.

The next step was the sale of those belongings that Frances did not want to ship back to America. Sonya's husband put an ad in the newspaper for the sale of household effects, and I started sorting and pricing items to be sold.

May 23rd, Wednesday

The bedlam of this day came after a sleepless night. My heart refused to leave Nakuru Memorial Hospital. The phone rang continually. Would-be buyers and the curious came by droves. Purchasers wanted to haggle over prices in the usual African style. Some bargained until I was exhausted, then left without buying. Others watched for a chance to *take* without paying. Not much sold that day.

In between, I packed two drums and contacted Dr. David Stuart, an English orthopedic surgeon who agreed to accept Bug as a patient if I could get him to Nairobi. When I phoned Dr. Malakooti, he said he would release him only if the Flying Doctor would transport him and then not before Friday.

Richard and John battled the mountain of red tape connected with Frances' taking Bill's body with her when she left on Saturday. We were all concerned for John. He could not turn his head and was in constant pain.

Two phone calls brightened the day with love: one from Cynthia Koen (South Africa) and the other from our son,

Dale, and his wife in California. Two bright spots in everyday were Jerri and Sonya standing by to help wherever a helping hand was needed.

May 24th, Thursday

John was supposed to go to Molo to collect Bug's and Bill's personal effects, but he was barely able to make short trips to offices in town. All of us felt that the grueling 250 miles would be more than he could bear. We welcomed advice that he could send Jerri with a letter, but how to go was the next question. The one car available was needed in Nairobi. Our prayer was answered by a new friend.

"If you need to go anyplace, my car and I are at your service."

They left me at Nakuru on the way so I could see Bug again. He was slightly improved but grieving over Bill's death. A large bouquet of gorgeous red roses, sent to him by another patient in the hospital, was a gesture of love that touched us both.

John phoned with good news. The Flying Doctor service could take Bug to Nairobi that afternoon. I got excited, but Dr. Malakooti was adamant. He felt it was a mistake to move him at all but, if we insisted, certainly not before the next day. I appreciated his concern but was sure that the transfer must be made.

It was so difficult to leave him again, but I was sustained by the promise of a ray of light in Nairobi for me by Friday afternoon.

On the way back, Jerri recounted her nerve-racking experience. First of all, there was the shock of the car still by the roadside with all the evidences of the horrible happening. She remembered that Don Fisher had asked for pictures, so she took some. The police at Molo handed her both men's billfolds and other items, then held out to her the pillow that had been Bug's prop. It was *still* wet with his blood. She nearly fainted as a wave of nausea swept over her. Recovering her balance, she asked them to please destroy it. She signed the record book and turned to leave.

The Sergeant said, "Oh, madam, here is something else for you to sign."

She asked, "What is this?"

He didn't answer. She wrote her name as he requested, took the piece of paper he handed her, and hurried away.

Later, when she showed me the paper, I was shocked. It was a notification of intention to prosecute John for violation of traffic regulations. I said, "Jerri, hide that paper. Under no circumstances must John see it. His good friend is dead and his supervisor critically injured. He has more than he can handle now. We'll show it to him later."

This is ahead of my story, but on February 9, 1974, we were driving from Mambasa to Nairobi, with all our thoughts focused on the court case two days later charging John with manslaughter. It was an afternoon of scattered showers, but we were able to see for miles in the freshly laundered atmosphere. A vista stretched before us of a dark cloud here and there spilling its contents and a rainbow or two glimmering briefly before dissolving.

One of the children said, "We have our own rainbow close to us." There was! We watched the end of it as it traveled with us for more than forty miles, parallel to the road. We saw each bush, rock, or bit of ground in its path touched with vibrant color for a few seconds as we moved along. There may be a scientific explanation, but I can only give you ours.

Bug said, "The first rainbow was a sign to Noah. This one is a sign to you, John. Quit worrying—this is a promise of victory."

But when John stood in the dock and the charges against him were read, it was a heart-chilling moment.

"You drove at a high speed and in a reckless, dangerous manner, causing the death of two people."

The public prosecutor claimed eleven witnesses to this fact, but John's lawyer had leverage with the manner in which the notice of intention to prosecute had been delivered. The law stated it must be delivered to the person concerned within fourteen days of issue. It was handed to Jerri without explanation. John didn't see it until a month later.

We won! And walked out of court with light footsteps and lighter hearts because John was cleared of all charges.

Now back to May 24, 1973.

Selling went better on our return—another drum packed, and we started on some boxes and the suitcases.

The Harris family lived in cramped, inadequate quarters, so they moved into the Cupples' house. It was a blessing.

May 25th, Friday

This was red letter day, but my excitement had to simmer under firm layers of "things that must be done." The hospital promised to let me know the time of Bug's arrival. I wanted so much to be there, but when no call came, I decided to phone them. On the third call, he was there. Ila took me to the hospital at once. He looked desperately weak and had been so heavily sedated for the trip that he was groggy. Most alarming was his left hand. It was swollen and almost black.

When the third drum was about half full, something happened I will never forget. I had marveled at the amazing strength granted me with so little sleep and no chance to rest, then, suddenly, it was gone. I felt like a deflated balloon and nearly fell headfirst into the drum. I hung onto the side of it and talked to my Friend.

"Lord, You have brought me this far—surely You will not forsake me now! Is there a lesson I must learn in this awful weakness?"

Then the vision came. I saw thousands upon thousands of God's children with their arms uplifted in prayer for us.

Jesus said, "That is your strength; you are upheld by the petitions of my people."

Strength returned as quickly as it had left. The drum was filled and sealed, and gratefully, I took another step up my stairway.

Today was Frances' last afternoon in Nairobi. I couldn't let her go to town alone. We worked off a long list, including cancellation of Bill's order for new glasses. Just after 5:00 P.M., we passed near the hospital. I wanted so much to stop, but some of the believers were waiting for us at the house, so we planned to return at the 7:00 P.M. visitation hour, bringing Frances and Eddie to see Bug.

What a shock! The room was empty when we arrived. His pajamas were lying in a heap on a chair. The nurse in charge said Dr. Stuart was doing emergency surgery. The laceration under his arm was badly infected, and the angle of the set needed changing. When I got over my initial dismay, I realized this was God's doing. When I saw him the first time at Nakuru, I knew the arm should be set differently for future leverage. Feebly, the praises started again.

May 26th, Saturday

How I longed that a plane would leave on time—for once. The whole journey would be a nightmare for Frances, and any delay would only intensify the horror. We stayed with her as long as we could, and waited on the waving deck for a last good-bye when she went to board the plane—nearly two hours late.

A biting, cold wind made us numb as we waited. I was to spend the morning with Bug, for in the afternoon buyers were coming to collect the purchases that would finish emptying the house. When I reached the hospital, I felt worse than many of the patients I saw—weary to the bone, aching chest, and throbbing head. I didn't want Bug to know, for his misery was so much greater than mine. But I've never been able to hide anything from him. When he started praying for *me* in a weak whisper, it broke my heart. He ended with "Ebenezer, hitherto the Lord has helped us." Then he asked, "Did she get off?"

I answered, "Yes," and laid my head on the side of his bed and passed out.

I awoke refreshed. When John came for me, a young couple from Ghana, the Dillards, were with him. We went to the hotel for lunch. While I appreciated the stew, it was gone, and a change was welcome. Back at the house, I struggled with the phone, trying to get through to the Allards in Ghana. I heard them say "Hello," and that was all. I didn't know until later that they heard the message I kept repeating.

By night, the only thing left in the house, besides the things to be shipped, was a chaise lounge that I could use for a bed. John brought David, his eleven-year-old son, and a cot so I would not be alone for the night.

May 27th, Sunday

I spent the morning at the hospital—my first opportunity to do some small things for my darling. I rubbed his cold feet, massaged his back, and read to him. I was thankful for a chance to talk to Dr. Stuart. According to him, Bug was not out of danger, but there was a chance for survival. "It will be a long, long road if he makes it." I clung to the comfort of knowing One who could alter and shorten roads.

The afternoon was spent filling the last two drums and boxing the rest of the freight. John and Tom Dillard moved everything to the garage, and I swept and cleared away rubbish. It was easier staying busy. A phone call from my daughter, Sharon, helped break the loneliness. There was just me and echoing memories in the big, empty house that night. It would have been a miserable time without communion with my Friend.

"Remember your all-night prayer in Ghana?"

"That was so strange—how could I forget? I have often wondered about the meaning of those three distinct burdens."

"You still don't understand? The first burden was for John, the second for Bug, and the third for Bill. And the answer for him was 'No.' Do not grieve because he was taken. Bill's work was done, and ten men will be so touched by his going that they will answer the call for laborers. Cannot ten do more than one?"

Oh, it was a beautiful night!

May 28th, Monday

The floors were washed and waxed early. John brought Jonathan and Jodi to stay with me when school was out.

Eventually, three loads were delivered in between showers of rain and the confusion that goes with moving.

"Has anyone seen the cuckoo clock's pendulum?"

"Where are the bolts for the big bed?"

"Motherrrrr! I can't find a shirt!"

I had a few pleasant moments' interlude when Sandra phoned. I had not seen Bug since Sunday morning, so I couldn't report much. I didn't tell her how uneasiness had tried to gnaw on me all day long.

We took a break and went to the hospital at 7:00 P.M. The day had been terrible for Bug; the upper portion of his body was burning with fever while his feet and legs were aching cold. The doctor said severe infection caused the high temperature and acute anemia the chilliness. He didn't look like he needed visitors, so we didn't stay long, but our prayer together was sweet. I suddenly realized that the bland, starchy hospital diet worked against his hypoglycemia. He needed protein, as well as prayer!

"John, could we take him a steak tomorrow?"

He agreed. "That's a good idea!"

That night, John reached the breaking point. Bill was gone; Bug still critical. John had pushed himself almost beyond endurance with the uninterrupted pain of his own injuries. Finally, it all came home to him. He walked the floor with tears rolling down his face. He could not be comforted. Jerri and I tried in vain to calm and reassure him. She whispered to me, "Please do something."

Guidance came. I closed the door to the living room and, in the hall, quietly placed a call to Tom Fred Tenney, our Foreign Missions Director.

"Brother Tenney, we have a man here who needs help."

When I explained, he exclaimed, "Amazing! Fifteen

minutes ago I predicted to Don this would happen. I have the answer. Put him on."

I opened the door and said without explanation, "Telephone, John."

That did it. The call and a tape. During the night I heard, at times, repeated snatches of a song—something about ". . . I'll stroll over heaven with you."

"Sorry I gave everyone such a bad time last night, Sister Freeman," John grinned sheepishly the next morning. "It's all right now. Brother Tenney encouraged me so much, and then I found this song and played it for hours." He played it again, and at the end he turned to me with shining eyes. "Someday I'll take a walk with my buddy up there, and we can talk it over. But 'til then, I'm not going to worry about it anymore."

May 29th, Tuesday

I went to town with John and the Dillards, who were leaving, and took a taxi to the hospital. They wouldn't let me go to Bug's room, so I wrote letters and waited.

Dr. Stuart talked to me a few minutes. He was quite gloomy and evasive about Bug's condition. He said they would change the cast and take out the stitches on the fourth of June, and he hoped by then they could tell how much longer he would have to be in the hospital.

He started to leave, then turned back and told me in considerable technical details all the conditions complicating Bug's recovery. And *if* he lived, I must plan for a long stay in Nairobi, for his ultimate recovery would be long and tedious.

I put my handkerchief over my mouth and praised the Lord silently while the doctor spelled out the grim facts. He looked at me quizzically. "Mrs. Freeman, I don't think you heard what I've said."

I moved the handkerchief. "Oh yes, Doctor, I heard every word, and thanks for telling me exactly the way it is."

John brought Bug a steak at noon. I cut it into small bites and coaxed part of it down, but he was too weak to chew very much. We resolved to get one for him every day.

I phoned Paul Box for word of Frances' flight and Bill's funeral. The Doug Davis family had met her and Eddie at John F. Kennedy Airport and helped them board their plane for Memphis. There they were met by a host of family and friends, including Brother Tenney. The funeral was made remarkable by a sweet Spirit and the assemblage of about 1,500 friends, 150 of them preachers.

Jerri went with us to the hospital at seven. When I opened the door to Bug's room, I didn't recognize him—he had deteriorated so much since that morning.

"That's not Bug, Jerri; they've moved him." I closed the door.

She said, "Let's be sure," and opened the door again. We tiptoed to the bedside. It was him, but he looked life-less. He couldn't even open his eyes or indicate whether he knew we were there or not. A nurse suggested we not stay long.

We left to meet the Kirbys and their replacement, the Johnsons, for dinner. The Johnsons had already proven to be steadfast friends, which they have continued to be, and the fellowship was great. But I could hardly wait to get home. I was in my room before 9:00 P.M.

"Dear Friend, You said if I would praise You, there would be victory. Bug seems farther from victory than ever, but I'm going to praise You according to Your Word. Thank

You, Lord, that his condition is critical."

I walked the floor and worshiped until my strength was gone. I alternated sitting and lying on the floor, but the praises rolled continually without slack. I heard Jerri's cuckoo clock marking the hours; that's how I know the miracle happened at 2:30 A.M. That was when the whole room suddenly lit up with a supernatural light so bright I opened my Bible and read Psalm 149. Slowly the light faded, but faith grew brighter. I stood and lifted my arms.

"Dearest Jesus, thank You for that lovely assurance. Forgive my desperation last night. Now I know the victory is sure. I planned to praise You all night, but today is another busy one, so I will sleep now."

And I did—sweetly.

May 30th, Wednesday

When I came out of my room about 7:00 A.M., John was pacing up and down the hall.

"I thought you were going to sleep all day, and I'm anxious to tell you something."

"Yes, John?"

"You keep on saying Brother Freeman will make it, and I've tried to believe, but when I saw him last night, I almost gave up hope. I came home determined to pray for him all night. He has been like a father to me. We missionaries need him—Africa needs him! I was on my knees praying and pleading with God to spare him. It was 2:30 this morning . . . I heard Jerri's clock . . . and . . ." he paused. "You won't believe this, but suddenly there was a bright light in my room. Now I *know* everything will be all right."

"I believe you, John. That same light shone in my room, and I believe it was shining on Bug, too. I'll ride with you to

Westlands when you take the schoolchildren to the bus and get a taxi on to the hospital. If you can manage, bring him another steak at noon, please."

The nurse asked me to wait, and I did—for over an hour. I wrote five letters and did a lot of praising Jesus. Finally, they said I could go in. Bug sat on the side of the bed, bright-eyed and alert.

"Good morning, hon! Did you bring the tape recorder?"

"Well, er . . . no, I didn't think about it." I looked at him in amazement and thought, "Last night you couldn't even open your eyes, much less your mouth, and now you need a tape recorder! This is wonderful!"

Then, the orders came thick and fast, and I was delighted.

"Clean my glasses, please, and pull me up by my good arm and help me walk around to get strength back in my legs. All this lying in bed makes a man weak."

"Help me walk to the wash basin."

"Bring the tape recorder this afternoon. I need to send a report to Brother Tenney."

"Get some nice 'thank you' cards, and send them to all the wonderful people who have been so helpful."

"I must go back to the hospital at Nakuru to thank the doctor and the nurses. They were unusually kind and considerate of me."

"I want to show you the flamingoes at Lake Nakuru."

"I want to go fishing at Lake Navasha."

"Phone South Africa to get the envelopes addressed for a PIM letter."

"Yes, yes, honey. We'll do it all," I interrupted. "But there's one thing I want you to do right now. Tell me *how* it happened. I know *when*, but I want to know *how!*"

"Well, the nurse came to see about me in the night. I pointed at her wrist for her to tell me the time. She said it was 2:00 A.M. I was terribly weak; I thought I must be near the end of the road. Twenty or thirty minutes later, however, I felt Jesus standing by my bed. I couldn't see Him, but I knew he was there and thought He had come to take me home. Instead, I felt something being pumped into my body. I've never had a blood transfusion, but somehow I knew I was receiving blood. Good blood! My head quit throbbing and became cool; my feet and legs got warm, and strength came."

We praised the Lord together. Dr. Stuart cleared his throat beside us. I opened my eyes, and he was beaming.

"I'm afraid I made you unhappy yesterday, Mrs. Freeman, but I think I can make you glad today. Something happened in this room in the early hours of the morning that we can neither account for nor explain. But because of that, the reverend should be able to travel in a week."

He went on to explain about removing stitches and a new cast. I was overjoyed that Bug would be out of the hospital in a week, then I realized—he means we can go *home*! My stairway had been long, tedious, and sometimes terrifying. My pace was often a slow crawl, but now I felt I was leaping with hind's feet. Magnify the Lord, O my soul!

The rest of the climb was not all made leaping, but the light lasted all the way!

We went home June 7. Three orthopedic surgeons in Pretoria agreed with Doctor Stuart and the two general practitioners in Kenya that the use of Bug's left arm was irrevocably lost. But God's promise of victory *through* praise was fulfilled beyond medical possibilities and even my highest hopes.

Blow by Blow

Three months after the accident, we were in Kenya again. Bug preached, went fishing at Lake Navasha, and helped unpack crates.

A complete examination with X-rays one year later left specialists astounded by the amazing mobility of the injured arm, even with the small amount of elbow bone structure remaining.

> *This is "our" story,*
> *This is our song,*
> *Praising our Savior*
> *All the day long!*

John Harris and Bug—taken three months
to the day after their accident in Kenya.

Tip #1

How to fit 103 books in a briefcase

Solution:
The Pentecostal Digital Reference Library

Now you can buy 103 Pentecostal books on 3 CDs. They are fully searchable and printable and work on both PC and Mac. Buying these books individually would cost almost $1000. They can be yours for less then $200. For more information or to purchase these valuable resources contact the Pentecostal Publishing House at 314-837-7300 or check us out online at PentecostalPublishing.com.